Allowance for Funds
Used during Construction

Allowance for Funds
Used during Construction
Theory and Application

Lawrence S. Pomerantz
and
James E. Suelflow

1975
MSU Public Utilities Studies

Institute of Public Utilities
Division of Research
Graduate School of Business Administration
Michigan State University

The Institute of Public Utilities, Graduate School of Business Administration, Michigan State University, publishes books, monographs, and occasional papers as part of its program of promoting academic interest in the study of public utilities and regulation. The views and opinions expressed in these works are solely those of the authors, and acceptance for publication does not constitute endorsement by the Institute, its member companies, or Michigan State University.

ISBN: 0-87744-135-9
Library of Congress Catalog Card No: 75-620097

Printed in the United States of America

Contents

v

List of Tables

List of Figures and Exhibits

Acknowledgments

The utility industry currently is burdened with immense economic and financial problems. These are caused by continuing increases in demands for services, shortages of inputs, high costs of money, and other inflationary pressures as they affect both construction and operations. As these utilities face unprecedented large construction programs, many of which may extend over a decade, in an environment pervaded by the above conditions, economic regulation and accounting principles developed to identify and overcome these conditions assume an added importance.

Within this framework lies the discussion at hand—allowance for funds used during construction. The amount of the allowance as it appears in the company's financial statements has raised a number of fundamental problems and questions, the answers to which are not easily found. (Yet, they should be available in both economic and accounting theory.) This, then, is the objective of this book: to advance sound suggestions to those who encounter the above problems.

No book is only the product of its authors; rather, it is the labor of many. Certain of these stand out for special recognition: Professor Harry M. Trebing and the Institute of Public Utilities provided both encouragement and financial support in making the initial part of this study a reality; Mid-Continent Telephone Corporation provided valuable uninterrupted blocks of time for the authors to work together; Mr. John Kluberg, Senior Vice-President, Consumers Power Company, provided extremely helpful criticism and suggestions throughout the study. To these individuals and others we are most appreciative. We also would like to thank Mr. Michael Champley for his time spent in the collection and analysis of the industry statistical data. Heartfelt thanks go to Mrs. Anita Goldman, who somehow skillfully managed to devote substantial amounts of time to the typing of several drafts of the manuscript while still performing her duties as secretary to four professors. Finally, to our editor, Ms. Elizabeth Johnston, goes special recognition for correction of tenses, unsplitting of infinitives, and other editorial skills on style and clarity so necessary to make it all hang together. Any errors and omissions must, of course, be ours.

1

Introduction

The decade of the 1960s witnessed the beginning of unprecedented increases in demands for all types of public utility services. Increases were particularly high in the electric utility field, as evidenced by brownouts, blackouts, and voltage reductions in many areas where supply failed to meet immediate demands. As a result, utilities began extremely large construction programs extended in many cases over periods of five to ten years and requiring vast amounts of both internal and external funding. In addition, environmental requirements and inflationary pressures have increased the burden of electric company construction costs beyond any previous level.

Investor-owned electric utilities are expected to spend nearly $88.1 billion for new facilities for the five-year period 1974–1978.[1] Table 1 illustrates the total actual and/or estimated construction bill on a year-by-year basis from 1974 through 1978 and also indicates the annual changes, which average approximately 6.9 percent. While some funds for this new construction will be generated internally, the greater portion will come from external sources—long-term debt and preferred and common

---

[1] Mitchell, Hutchins, Inc., *Electric Power Industry Outlook: Status Report*, 6 November 1974, p. 2.

stocks. Table 2 specifies the sources of all funds based on the indicated construction expenditures given in Table 1. One notices immediately the minor role of equity funding and that the great proportion of funding will come from long-term debt. This is occurring at a time when debt costs, as well as construction costs, are at unprecedented heights, which is the case whether one uses figures that are absolute or relative to the size of existing facilities. The average annual construction cost index increased 5.4 percent from 1965 through 1972, and from 1969 to 1972 at the rate of 7.1 percent annually. Such inflationary rates have

TABLE 1.   Construction Expenditures for Investor-Owned Electric Utilities

Year	Generation ($billions)	Transmission ($billions)	Distribution ($billions)	Other ($billions)	Total[a] ($billions)	Percentage change
1978[b]	12.5	2.1	5.1	1.2	20.9	11.2
1977[b]	11.1	1.9	4.7	1.1	18.8	11.2
1976[b]	9.9	1.8	4.2	1.0	16.9	5.6
1975[b]	8.8	2.8	3.5	0.9	16.0	3.2
1974[b]	8.7	2.2	3.7	0.8	15.5	3.3
1973	8.8	2.0	3.4	0.7	15.0	—

SOURCE: Mitchell, Hutchins, Inc., *Electric Power Industry Outlook: Status Report,* 6 November 1974, p. 3.
[a] Totals may not add due to rounding.
[b] Estimates.

raised capacity costs per kilowatt to staggering levels. As a result, utilities are demanding higher and higher consumer prices. Furthermore, the financial world has expressed concern for the utilities' ability to show sufficient income levels to maintain interest coverages and protect bond ratings.

NATURE OF THE PROBLEM

During periods of heavy construction and expansion, a primary concern to utility management, investment analysts, and regulators is the increasing amount and impact of allowances for funds used during construction (AFC) on firms' financial status.[2] Whether viewed from the

---

[2] "Allowance for funds used during construction" is now widely used by electric utilities in place of the original term, "Interest during construction," in accordance

TABLE 2. Projected Construction Expenditures, Internal Cash Generation, and External Capital Needs of Investor-Owned Electric and Gas Utilities, 1973–1978, in Billions of Dollars

Year	Construction, elec. + gas = tot.	Internal sources			External sources	
		Retained earnings	Depreciation	Deferrals and cash adjust's	Indicated new financing*	Expected common stock financing
1978E	$21.3	$2.4	$5.0	$2.0	$12.0	$2.5
1977E	19.3	2.1	4.5	1.8	10.9	2.3
1976E	17.5	1.7	4.2	1.7	9.9	2.2
1975E	16.7	1.5	3.8	1.6	9.8	2.2
1974E	16.3	1.3	3.4	1.0	10.6	1.9
1973	15.7	1.4	3.0	0.9	10.3	2.6

SOURCE: Mitchell, Hutchins, Inc., Electric Power Industry Outlook: Status Report, 6 November 1974, pp. 4–5.
*Totals may not add due to rounding.

vantage of the accountant, the economist, the financial analyst, the Securities and Exchange Commission, the Federal Power Commission, or the state regulatory agencies, the concern is clearly evident. For example, in a speech before the New York Society of Security Analysts, Mr. Richard Walker, managing partner of the Regulated Industries Division of Arthur Andersen & Company, cited a survey of 20 investor-owned utilities on the magnitude of AFC as a part of net income. The results of the survey showed that in 1968 the AFC credit to income was 10 percent or more of net income in 29 percent of the companies; in 1969, 42 percent reported similar contributions to income.[3]

This growth in the amounts of capitalized AFC is further evidenced when analyzing Class A and Class B electric utilities as a group; in 1966 AFC represented an amount equal to 4.6 percent of net income, while in 1972 this percentage had increased to approximately 24.2 percent.[4] A study of selected electric utilities shows that in 1974 the major firms derived an average of 40 percent of their income from AFC, compared to only 4 percent in 1965 and 20 percent in 1970.[5] More specifically, two utilities, Duke Power and Virginia Electric and Power, derived 81 percent and 78 percent, respectively, of their 1974 net income available for common stockholders from this source.[6] With such large percentages of net income emanating from AFC, concern has been expressed about the reduction in the "quality" of the utility's earnings.[7] Mr. Walker testified in a hearing before the Florida Public Service Commission on

---

with FPC *Order No. 436*, issued in August 1971. "Allowance for funds used during construction" (AFC) is the term used throughout this study. Other writers have abbreviated the term to ADC and AFUDC.

[3] Richard Walker, "Interest During Construction Credits in the Utility Industry," paper presented to the New York Society of Security Analysts, New York, 30 November 1970, p. 10.

[4] Federal Power Commission (hereafter FPC), *Statistics of Privately Owned Electric Utilities in the United States, 1972, Class A and B* (hereafter *Statistics*) (Washington, D.C.: U.S. Government Printing Office, 1973), Table 12, p. XXVI, and Table 12a, p. XXVII.

[5] Hornblower and Weeks, Hemphill, Noyes, *Electric Utility Industry Perspective*, August 1975, p. 6; and *Forbes* 112 (1 November 1973): 41.

[6] Hornblower and Weeks, *Perspective*, p. 6.

[7] *Forbes* 112 (1 November 1973): 41; and John C. Burton, "Some General and Specific Thoughts on the Accounting Environment," *Journal of Accountancy* 136 (October 1973): 46.

18 June 1973 regarding ratemaking treatment of construction work in progress and AFC. At that time he stated: "Investors apparently do not value a dollar of earnings from the allowance for funds charged to construction as much as they do a dollar of earnings from operations for, in this sense, they view it as being of lesser quality than cash flow earnings.[8]

A similar conclusion was reached by Mr. W. T. Hyde, economist and public utility consultant, when he testified before the North Carolina Utilities commission: "Investors can hardly be expected to give much value to earnings so heavily dependent on the credit for interest charged to construction which results from nothing more than an arbitrary credit and an assumption that the plant under construction will produce sufficient earnings to offset the decline in this credit when the plant is placed in service. This is a highly speculative and problematical assumption."[9]

Mr. Charles A. Benore, currently of Mitchell, Hutchins, Inc., a securities investment firm, also has expressed his concern: "Currently, about four out of five investors that I consult with appear to believe that AFC earnings are inferior to operating earnings."[10] He further pointed out that the amount of AFC is not a current cash flow which is needed to pay dividends.[11] In fact, the authors' study confirms this view; in 1972 we found that 29 Class A and B public utilities paid dividends of which at least 6 percent and as high as 86 percent came from AFC credits. In other words, these firms operated under conditions where cash flow earnings from operations available to common stockholders were only 14–94 percent of the actual dividends paid.[12]

The SEC has expressed its deep concern by requiring that full disclosure of AFC be contained on prospectuses of electric utility registrants that are filed before them. The disclosure required reads substantially as follows:

---

[8] Richard Walker, "Testimony and Exhibits of Richard Walker for Arthur Andersen & Co.," Florida Public Service Commission Docket No. 72609-PU, 18 June 1973.

[9] Affidavit by Mr. W. Truslo Hyde, Jr., filed with the North Carolina Utilities Commission in *Re Duke Power Co.* Docket No. E-7, Sub 128, cited in ibid., p. 7.

[10] Paper presented at the *Electrical World* Utility Executive Conference, 7 June 1973, cited in ibid., p. 6.

[11] Ibid., p. 6.

[12] Authors' calculation based on FPC, *Statistics.*

The allowance for funds used during construction, an item of nonoperating income, is defined in the applicable regulatory system of accounts as the net cost for the period of construction of borrowed funds used for construction purposes and a reasonable rate upon other funds when so used. The allowance for funds used during construction amounted to __%, __%, __%, __%, and __% of net income available for common stock for the years ____, ____, ____, ____, ____, and __% for the __ months ended ____, respectively. The allowance rate for the cost of funds used during construction has increased from __% in ____ to __% in ____ and thereafter. The amount of the allowance as a percentage of net income available for common stock has increased substantially since ____ principally as a result of substantial increases in construction work in progress aid in the costs of capital.[13]

Underlying this statement is the SEC concern that significant amounts of current income do not represent cash earnings. Thus, the rate at which AFC is calculated represents a "hoped-for" return to be allowed in the future. Because of commission regulation, there is no certainty that such earnings ever will be forthcoming or, if they are, it may be in the distant future when inflation will take its toll on the real income of the utility.

Finally, the FPC in a proposed rule-making announcement has requested interested parties to comment on its proposal to modify the instructions and accounts of those utilities under its jurisdiction. The proposal would allow the inclusion of construction work in progress in the rate bases of electric and gas utilities in order to increase immediate cash flows.[14]

While AFC calculated on debt capital can be justified as a construction cost such as that of brick and mortar, AFC calculated on equity funding may be in the realm of abstract thinking. Although these earnings may be acceptable in an economic sense, they may not fit the traditional concept of income in an accounting sense. There is ample support in economic theory for paying interest on capital invested in construction costs of production facilities prior to their producing con-

---

[13] As expressed in a letter dated 6 March 1973 to Consumers Power Company of Jackson, Michigan, by William J. Kurz, Branch Chief, SEC, Washington, D.C.

[14] Federal Power Commission, Docket No. RM75-13, *Construction Work in Progress*, 14 November 1974.

sumer goods or services.[15] Conventional accounting, however, does not provide a positive theory of anticipated revenue.[16] "The accountant would normally say that income is only earned when revenues flow from the assets created by the investment capital."[17] Since there are no current cash flows from AFC, any increase in income for dividends due to AFC must be recognized as income not provided through the normal process of providing utility services. Furthermore, as mentioned above, the lack of cash flow has given the electric utilities an added problem with interest coverages as they may be specified in indenture covenants. "Typical utility mortgage restrictions permit only 15% of AFC to be used to cover interest payments."[18] Bond ratings also may suffer as coverages decline and as AFC becomes a greater portion of income.

BACKGROUND AND PURPOSE OF THE STUDY

In accounting for AFC, the problems of the electric utilities are more numerous and complex than are those of unregulated industrial and commercial enterprises. This is due primarily to the inherent differences in both the nature of operations of regulated and unregulated enterprise and the environment within which each operates.

Some of the economic and physical characteristics basic to public utilities, and to this study of AFC, that distinguish them from other types of enterprises are presented below. In addition, several important aspects of utility regulation, in particular, the role of utility accounting regulation, will be discussed. To an extent, the discussion of AFC as it applies to public utilities must consider economic theory, regulation, and accounting theory and practice.

Economic Importance of Plant Investment

The typical public utility is a vertically integrated, monopolistic enterprise which both produces and distributes its service. In addition, compared to most other unregulated businesses, public utilities require a large investment in fixed plant and equipment relative to annual rev-

---

15 See chapter 2, below.
16 *Journal of Accountancy* 136 (October 1973): 46.
17 Ibid.
18 *Forbes* 112 (1 November 1973): 42.

enues produced. As a result, public utilities (1) constantly need new facilities and are heavily engaged in large capital expenditure programs;
(2) constantly need capital funds for fixed investment; (3) incur a relatively high percentage of fixed costs, such as interest, depreciation, and
property taxes; and (4) must give more attention to accounting for
plant costs rather than such costs as those of labor and inventory.

The Role of Regulation

It has been said that regulation accomplishes the same goals for the
monopolistic public utilities that competition achieves for unregulated
competitive enterprises. More specifically: Regulation (1) seeks to prevent utilities from charging unreasonably high or low prices; (2) seeks to
assure adequate earnings by utilities so as to promote adequate expansion to meet consumer demand; (3) seeks to provide consumers with
maximum service at the lowest possible prices; (4) often attempts to
promote the development of a certain industry or region; (5) attempts
to set price at levels sufficiently high to discourage unnecessary or wasteful consumption of scarce resources; and (6) may be designed to ensure maximum public safety.[19] Success in meeting the first two objectives
is heavily dependent upon the use of accounting data. In regulating
prices and earnings, commissions have established the uniform system
of accounts to serve as a basic standard in carrying out the rate regulation function.

The two main aspects of rate regulation are the setting of revenue
requirements of a utility, known as the general rate level, and the approval of specific rates to charge the customer utilizing utility services,
also known as the rate structure. It is the first of these aspects which is
relevant to our discussion. Capitalized AFC is an element of plant cost
which eventually enters a utility's rate base. To this extent, the capitalization of AFC practiced by electric utilities is more than a problem
of accounting.

The Role of Accounting

Regulatory accounting is the yardstick by which the commissions can

---

[19] Charles F. Phillips, Jr., *The Economics of Regulation*, rev. ed. (Homewood, Ill.:
Richard D. Irwin, 1969), p. 124.

measure and control the various aspects of rate regulation, such as determining the utility's cost of service. Commissions, through the systems
of accounts, use accounting as an aid in determining whether a utility
(1) accurately records its operating expenses, depreciation, taxes, and
plant and investment; (2) distinguishes properly between capital and
revenue expenditures; (3) properly separates its utility from its nonutility business; and (4) charges its customers reasonable rates.[20]

The uniform systems of accounts, as prescribed by the various regulatory bodies, represent an effective means of communicating financial
information between the utility companies and all interested parties. A
system of accounts is more than a listing of balance sheet and income
statement accounts in which the public utilities record transactions. It
also usually contains (1) a definition of each account along with instructions as to the types of transaction to be recorded, (2) statements
as to the bases to be utilized in determining amounts that may be recorded in the accounts, (3) a listing of general definitions and instructions, and (4) the general form and sequence of the major financial
statements.[21]

Exhibit 1 provides a graphic illustration of a typical system of accounts which might be prescribed by a state or federal regulatory commission for an electric utility. It is adapated from the Federal Power
Commission's uniform system of accounts for Class A and B electric
utilities.[22] The framework shown in Exhibit 1 also represents the order
and scheme of items presented in a public utility balance sheet and
income statement. Any subsequent general references made in this study
to "the systems of accounts" or utility "financial statements" will refer
to this framework unless specifically noted otherwise.

Historical evidence confirms that the AFC capitalization practice was
first adopted into the scheme of public utility accounting by railroads in
the 1840s.[23] The practice also was being used by electric utilities prior to

20 Ibid., pp. 144–45.
21 James E. Suelflow, *Public Utility Accounting: Theory and Application*, MSU Public Utilities Studies (East Lansing: Division of Research, Michigan State University, 1973), chapters 2 and 3.
22 FPC, *Uniform System of Accounts Prescribed for Public Utilities and Licensees*
(hereafter *Uniform System*) (Washington, D.C.: U.S. Government Printing
Office, January 1973).
23 J. B. Madigan, "Depreciation and Other Aspects of Interest-During-Construction,"
Proceedings of the National Conference of Electric and Gas Utility Accountants
(Washington, D.C.: 1965), p. F 43.

EXHIBIT 1. **A Typical System of Accounts for Public Utilities**

BALANCE SHEET ACCOUNTS
(100–299)

ASSETS AND OTHER DEBITS
(100–199)

101–120 Utility Plant
121–128 Other Property and Investments
131–174 Current and Accrued Assets
181–188 Deferred Debits

LIABILITIES AND OTHER CREDITS
(201–299)

201–217 Proprietary Capital
221–224 Long-term Debt
231–242 Current and Accrued
         Liabilities
251–256 Deferred Credits
261–265 Operating Reserves
   271 Contributions in Aid of
        Construction
281–283 Accumulated Deferred
        Income Taxes

RETAINED EARNINGS ACCOUNT
(436–439)

   216 Unappropriated R/E (at
        beginning of period)
   433 Balance Transferred
        from Income
   436 Appropriations of R/E
        Net Additions to R/E
437–438 Dividends Declared
   439 Adjustments to R/E
   216 Unappropriated R/E (at
        end of period)

INCOME ACCOUNTS
(400–435)

UTILITY OPERATING INCOME
(400–414)
400 Operating Revenues

      Operating Expenses
401 Operating Expense
402 Maintenance Expense
403 Depreciation Expense
404–407 Amortization Expense
408 Taxes Other than
      Income Taxes
409 Income Taxes
410 Provision for Deferred
      Income Taxes
411 Income Taxes Deferred
      in Prior Years—Cr.
      Total Utility Operating
      Expenses
      Net Operating Revenues
412–414 Other Operating Income
      Net Utility Operating Income
415–421.1 Other Income
421.2–426 Other Income Deductions
408–420 Taxes Applicable to Other
      Income Deductions
427–431 Interest Charges
434–435 Extraordinary Items
  409.3 Net Income

NOTE: Based on Federal Power Commission, *Uniform System of Accounts Prescribed for Public Utilities and Licensees* (Washington, D.C.: U.S. Government Printing Office, 1973).

the 1908 issuance of the first uniform systems of accounts prescribed for them.[24] The initial systems of accounts, adopted in 1908 by the states of New York and Wisconsin, also provided for the capitalization of AFC, but in a somewhat restrictive manner. Apparently, interest capitalization was allowed only on debt obligations: "Charge to this account (Interest during construction—undistributed plant) the interest accrued upon all monies (and credits available upon demand) acquired for use in connection with the construction and equipment of the property from the time of such acquisition until the construction is ready for use."[25]

In 1920, however, the National Association of Railroad and Utilities Commissioners (NARUC[26]) recommended a system of accounts for electric utilities which contained the following provisions with regard to capitalizing AFC:

> When any bonds, notes or other evidences of indebtedness are sold, or any interest-bearing debt is incurred for acquisition and construction of original road and equipment, extension, additions, and betterments, the interest accruing on the part of the debt representing the cost of property chargeable to road and equipment accounts (less interest, if any, allowed by depositaries on unexpended balances) after such funds become available for use and before the receipt or the completion or coming into service of the property so acquired shall be charged to this account.

> When such securities are sold at a premium the proportion of such premium assignable to the time between the date of the actual issuance of the securities and the time when the property acquired or the improvement made becomes available for service shall be credited to this account.

> This account shall also include such proportion of the discount and expense on funded debt issued for the acquisition of original road, original equipment, road extensions, additions, and betterments, as is equitably assignable to the period between the date of the actual issuance of securities and the time when the property acquired or the improvement made becomes available for the service

---

[24] Ferd Rydell, "Interest During Construction," Part I, *Public Utilities Fortnightly* 79 (11 May 1967): 42.

[25] A. W. Hatch, "Interest During Construction," *Proceedings of the National Conference of Electric and Gas Utility Accountants* (New York: 1952), p. 320.

[26] Now the National Association of Regulatory Utility Commissioners (NARUC).

for which it is intended. The proportion of discount and expense thus chargeable shall be determined by the ratio between the period to the completion or coming into service of the facilities or improvements acquired and the period of the entire life of the securities issued.

This account shall also include reasonable charges for interest, during construction period before the property becomes available for services, on the carrier's own funds expended for construction purposes.[27]

The NARUC system was the first to allow electric utilities to capitalize actual interest on borrowed funds and also capitalize imputed "interest" on other funds used during construction. Subsequent systems of accounts for these utilities have been revised considerably since the first NARUC adoption. However, the general principle of the provision for capitalizing AFC has remained unchanged.[28]

Today, for example, the FPC's uniform systems of accounts for Class A and B electric utilities, in Utility Plant Instruction 3, subparagraph (17), provides for the practice as follows: "Allowance for funds used during construction includes the net cost for the period of construction of borrowed funds used for construction purposes and a reasonable rate on other funds when so used. No allowance for funds used during construction shall be included in these accounts upon expenditures for construction projects which have been abandoned."[29]

Although public utilities have been capitalizing and recording AFC in their financial records for over a century, the accounting for these capitalized dollars has been a confused and often misunderstood subject. Until recently, because of its relative stability and insignificance, little attention was accorded AFC. In telephone and nonutility applications AFC still is not emphasized as much as it is in the electric utility situation. However, the dramatic changes in demand for services and subsequent construction projects have generated a great deal of concern and controversy regarding AFC, especially as it relates to the electric utilities. Accountants, economists, financial analysts, regulators, and utility managers have presented concepts and theories to support the practices used,

---

[27] Hatch, "Interest During Construction," pp. 320–21.
[28] Ibid.
[29] FPC, *Uniform System*, p. 101-7.

but those who must deal with this subject seldom are in accord regarding proper procedures.

While controversy rages, few have offered a concrete examination and analysis to resolve these misunderstandings. The purpose of this study is to provide an in-depth analysis of the allowance for funds used during construction as it applies to electric utilities and to offer practical suggestions for coping with the problems and questions which have arisen. The investigation and analysis, however, easily could be applied to the gas and telephone utilities as well.

TERMINOLOGY

Two concepts used in this study have varied meanings, depending upon their context. For this reason, it is important to set forth and clarify our definitions.

Imputed Interest

Imputed interest is defined as the cost for the use of any capital funds provided by other than a creditor group. Thus, imputed interest is to equity funds (including those internally generated) what contractural interest is to debt or creditor funds. The essential difference between contractual and imputed interest is the presence or absence of a contractual agreement and a liability. Note that the definition employed here differs from that of the Accounting Principles Board in *Opinion No. 21—Interest on Receivables and Payables*,[30] where *imputed interest* means an approximated interest amount.[31]

Allowance for Funds Used during Construction

The term "allowance for funds used during construction" has different conotations depending upon the circumstances in which it is used. Traditionally, when applied to regulated public utilities, the term includes both the actual interest cost of borrowed funds and the imputed

---

[30] Accounting Principles Board [hereafter APB], *Opinion No. 21—Interest on Receivables and Payables* (New York: American Institute of Certified Public Accountants [hereafter AICPA], August 1971), p. 421.
[31] Ibid.

"interest" on other funds used during construction. However, when applied to unregulated firms, the term includes only the actual interest cost on borrowed funds.

SUMMARY

As has been stated, the purpose of this study is to analyze and offer practical suggestions concerning the allowance for funds used during construction. This chapter has presented some general information, but for a fuller understanding the reader also must be aware of certain fundamental economic and accounting theories and concepts. The economic theory underlying investment, interest, and AFC is discussed in chapter 2. Chapter 3 presents a similar discussion from an accounting viewpoint. This background will provide the setting for the more effective discussion and analysis of AFC in chapters 4 through 7.

2

Economic Theory of
Investment and Interest Rates
Underlying Capitalization of AFC

The basis for public utilities being allowed to capitalize allowance for funds used during construction is established both in economic and accounting theory (see chapter 3). While AFC is not specifically discussed in general economic analysis, its economic basis emanates from the theory of investment and interest rates as these latter are related to and are part of the input in the cost-of-production theory of value. Therefore, it is fundamental to understand this theory in order to appreciate the economic rationale for capitalization of AFC.

THEORY OF VALUE

The three principal economic factors of production generally have been identified as land, labor, and capital (AFC relates specifically to the last). Since each involves a scarce resource, each has economic value and positive opportunity costs.[1] Therefore, each must receive adequate

---

[1] Opportunity cost is defined as the alternative investment opportunities having positive values or costs.

implicit or explicit compensation, the rate for which is determined by the pricing mechanism. The labor factor is paid for through wages, land is compensated by rental payments, and capital receives compensation through the payment of interest (part of which may be AFC). One of the first political economists to recognize this triad was J. B. Say, who, as early as 1803, had developed an approach explicitly based on these three factors of production. His contribution is significant here because he was the first of the classical economists to identify the role of the entrepreneur as separate from that of the capitalist. Say's analysis viewed the entrepreneurial function as one of combining the three factors and accounting for their costs, while the capitalist function was one of providing the funds. Most political economists did not make such a distinction until the late nineteenth century.[2]

Although some factor costs may be implicit, not represented by cash outlays, and not explicitly reflected in the utilities' accounts, they nevertheless must be recognized. Cognizance must be taken of the fact that, in a comparable firm, cash outlays result if labor (including management) is hired, land rented, and money borrowed. Whether implicit or explicit, such costs must be dealt with by economists. The value of all goods and services consumed are included in these costs, regardless of the actual outlay and whether or not the entrepreneur puts them into the records.

The economist's treatment of costs will differ to some extent from that of the accountant. Economists generally believe that recorded costs are incomplete. For example, interest is charged to the accounts of bonds outstanding and is recognized fully; however, the equity money invested by stockholders in the firm generally is held to earn "income," which is available for dividends and is viewed as profit. Economic theory would acknowledge all or part of the profit as an allocable cost, which, as a minimum, would be the going interest rate. The economist also recognizes a minimum inducement is needed to hold capital in the firm. This generally is identified as annual profit or the opportunity costs referred to above.

Another early economist, Frances A. Walker, recognized four specific claims on revenue: wages, rent, profits, and interest.[3] He noted that

[2] Eduard Heimann, *History of Economic Doctrines* (New York: Oxford University Press, 1964), p. 110.

[3] Francis Amasa Walker, *The Wages Question* (1876), in John Fred Bell, A *His-*

many earlier English economists discussed only the distribution of the first three. Thus, they combined two elements in the profit function: a return profit for the abstinence of the owner of the capital and the personal efforts of the employer of capital. To Walker, the second, or entrepreneurial, function had been inadequately treated or given only cursory recognition.[4]

In his *History of Economic Analysis,* Joseph Schumpeter also commented upon the failure of the classical economists to treat adequately the difference between capitalists and entrepreneurs.

> So far as the "classics," within the precincts of fundamental analysis, spoke of monetary interest at all, they did not mean a return on money loans per se, as did the scholastic writers, and as do some of us, but only a monetary expression for a return on physical capital that, moreover, was expressed in terms of money solely for the sake of convenience. Actually, as we know, their capital was goods.

> In the first place, since pure interest, if we neglect the interest on consumers' loans was nothing but the bulk of business profits, the fundamental problem was the explanation of those business profits: there was no *separate* problem of interest at all. . . . This was one of the results of the habit of identifying the roles of the industrialist and the capitalist, which subtly influenced the thought even of those who occasionally recognized the essential difference between them.[5]

J. B. Clark was able to provide a much more satisfactory theory of the entrepreneur's function and entrepreneurial gains.[6] Schumpeter believed "Clark's contribution was the most significant of all; he was the first to strike a novel note by connecting entrepreneurial profits, considered as a surplus over interest (and rent), with the successful introduction into the economic process of technological, commercial, or organizational improvements."[7]

---

tory of Economic Thought (New York: Ronald Press, 1953), pp. 505–12. Walker's textbook, *Political Economy* (1883), may have had considerable influence, as it was extremely popular.

[4] Ibid., p. 232.

[5] Joseph A. Schumpeter, *History of Economic Analysis* (New York: Oxford University Press, 1954), pp. 646–47.

[6] John Bates Clark, *Distribution of Wealth* (1899), in Schumpeter, *History,* p. 894.

[7] Schumpeter, *History,* p. 894.

In the twentieth century, more and more economists recognized interest as an entrepreneurial cost and separated out profits as a residual. Until that time the cost-of-production theory of value was not complete. A few economists were approaching the theory of value only from the demand side (that is, value in exchange), which subsequently resulted in the marginal utility theory. Alfred Marshall brought the two together and harmonized the utility concept (demand analysis) and the cost of production (supply analysis). He pointed out that value is almost entirely influenced by demand in the short run, but, in the long run, supply is also important; the price of a good or service cannot vary greatly from the cost incurred in producing it. Thus, at least from the economist's viewpoint, all goods and services consumed in the production process have a value and, therefore, a cost attached to them—in the context of our discussion, AFC.

The theory of value was the principal path of all the classical and neoclassical economists. Many of them were businessmen, well schooled in business affairs. They undoubtedly drew some of their ideas from existing business practice. At the same time, their writings probably had a reinforcing as well as a modifying effect upon existing and future business practices. Without question, their work on the cost-of-production theory of value influenced the "interest" issue during the late nineteenth and early twentieth century. Prior to 1880 there is little evidence that payments to equity holders for the use of funds presented any practical or theoretical accounting problems. The accountant was and still is more concerned with measuring costs by actual cash outlay, with some notable exceptions, such as depreciation.

Throughout the recorded history of economic activity men have attempted to explain their desires for immediate use of capital funds as opposed to the desire to postpone the use of those funds. From the consumer's viewpoint the choice is one of immediate satisfaction by utilizing funds to purchase final consumer goods or of foregoing immediate pleasure by saving and gaining satisfaction at some future date. In 1836, Nassau Senior expanded on the triad distribution theory by noting that capital is formed by "abstinence" from consumption and that this deserves payment as does labor. The reward is essentially one of time: "If employed for the purchase of consumers' goods, the money stimulates their production; if plowed back into production it redirects the factors of production into the production of capital goods whose ultimate consumable fruits will become more plentiful, but available only later. The sacrifice which requires compensation is one of time."[8] Business enterprises face a similar internal dilemma. Income and recaptured investment may be disposed of immediately through dividend or capital repayments to owners (stockholders), or satisfaction may be forestalled by retaining earnings and depreciation and reinvesting these funds in production facilities which, hopefully, will yield added future return. As long as investment already embedded is not returned to the lender (stockholder), even though depreciation is recorded, the lender expects interest, or a return, because of the positive time preference of anticipated future returns—once again relevant to the AFC concept. Recaptured investment through depreciation as well as retained earnings require a return (interest) until such time as plant is liquidated. Therefore, it is assumed that depreciation and retained earnings will be reinvested in the firm at a cost, and that cost or return is positive on these funds as well as others recently borrowed.

Whether for an individual or a business, the decision process of immediate or postponed consumption will be determined by the demand for and supply of funds provided through postponed satisfaction at the price (interest) the supplier is willing to accept and the demander is willing to pay. Diagrammatically, the supply of funds is a positively sloped function, with more funds being supplied as interest rates increase due to added risk and uncertainty. Likewise, the demand for funds is a negatively sloping function, with smaller amounts being taken at higher interest rates. Equilibrium rate i^* is shown in Figure 1: the point

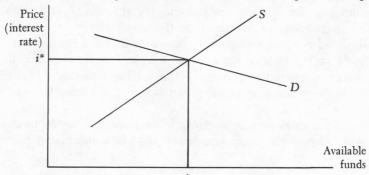

FIGURE 1.   The Supply of and Demand for Funds

---

[8] Nassau William Senior, *An Outline of the Science of Political Economy* (1836), in Heimann, *History*, p. 117.

at which lenders equate a positive time preference between immediate consumption and future satisfaction, and, similarly, the point at which entrepreneurs regard the cost (interest) on funds as just equal to the marginal return that can be expected from added investment.

Such economic analysis is at the very heart of the debate regarding the allowance for funds used during construction, that is, whether it is economically sound to impute a price (interest) to attract funds which are forestalled in the consumption-satisfaction process until the future date when the created physical capital assets will produce consumer satisfaction and to pay the price (sacrifice) which must be made for the waiting.

THE RATE OF INTEREST

It generally is conceded that the problems of determining capital requirements and the subsequent interest payments are more difficult to solve than those involved with most other production factors and their pricing. Risk and uncertainty generally are identified as the major stumbling blocks, as capital assets require long time periods to complete construction. This lengthy process prompted Marshall to use the word *waiting* as a reminder that the passage of time is of crucial importance when talking about capital and its costs.[9] This period of waiting is likened to having pleasure or satisfaction today as contrasted to the same benefits promised at some time in the future. Of particular importance to utilities is the lag between the time construction of the physical capital assets is begun and the time the new facilities are completely installed and consumer production begins. It is this detour in the production process which creates many of the problems or uncertainties in the theory of interest and capital. Unlike labor and land, the use of capital in the production process bears heavily upon temporal relationships.

A simple analogy may be worthwhile. In a one-commodity economy, the generation of electricity, the power could be consumed at the pro-

---

[9] Alfred Marshall, *Principles of Economics*, 8th ed. (London and New York: Macmillan, 1920), p. 233. Here *waiting* may be distinguished from *positive time* preference in that the latter assumes a positive interest factor functioning immediately, whereas waiting is a foregoing of any immediate return today for greater returns at a later date.

duction site and satisfaction gained immediately. However, if the producer and the investors are willing to forego payment or return from that immediate consumption, they may choose to utilize additional invested capital in constructing transmission and distribution facilities. This would be particularly advantageous to both parties if, through constructing such facilities, consumption of electrical energy increased several fold. The suppliers of funds have decided to "wait" and to forego immediate satisfaction (sales and returns today) for increased satisfaction (sales and returns) tomorrow. Uncertainty complicates the attempt to determine the present value of immediate sales versus the "prospective return" on foregone sales to be consummated in the future.

Another consideration which cannot be overlooked is the waiting period, which may be lengthened or shortened depending upon the elaborateness of the facilities to be constructed and qualities of materials used. It would be possible to construct a very inexpensive but short-lived transmission line to carry electricity to final consumers. Alternatively, the producer might decide to construct more durable facilities to reach more distant consumers, thus increasing the period of time during which the investor must wait for production of consumer electricity to begin. In this instance the "price" of waiting is important. Stated differently, once again the supply of capital or available funds depends heavily upon the cost of this capital or interest measured in terms of the preference to consume a small amount of electricity today or to wait for wider distribution and greater consumption tomorrow. From the viewpoint of demand, planners must decide whether the contemplated transmission-distribution system will offer greater productivity tomorrow and thus increase benefits to investors, or offer lower productivity today but provide immediate satisfaction. Before the electric utility can make its decision, the time preference involved in the investment must assure the investor that there will be a positive reward for postponing immediate production and sales. This reward is the "interest" demanded by the provider of capital. Quite simply, the present value of future returns discounted at an acceptable interest rate must be determined. If the present value of expected net future returns compares favorably with the present cost of the production facilities, then the decision to invest also must be accompanied by a decision to refrain from current consumption—waiting.

While the above is an unembellished illustration of the utilization of capital and its payment in the overall production process, a complete understanding requires an elaboration of several concepts. First, a determination must be made of how investments actually are carried out in a modern capitalistic economy. Second, it is necessary to discover how the return on capital is calculated. Finally, one must identify ways in which the return can be compared to a cost of the capital asset.

In any modern capitalistic economy one must accept the fact that, as a general rule, a decision to wait or refrain from immediate consumption and the decision to invest may not be part of the thought processes of the same person. For analysis, two assumptions are required. First, assume that all money which is saved at a given rate of interest immediately will be invested in capital assets. Second, assume that the demand for capital assets is entirely separate from the supply of savings which were used to purchase these assets.

Turning first to demand considerations, it is quite apparent that capital assets will be demanded only if they produce final goods for consumption which have a revenue potential. As does any factor of production, any new demand for added capital assets, in the long run, will have a marginal revenue product (MRP) curve or schedule attached to it. That schedule will measure the feasibility of the addition of the new capital assets plus the other factors of production in order to calculate the total additional revenue (MRP) which the firm might anticipate receiving. These revenues must cover both the repayment of the funds borrowed to purchase the capital assets plus the "rent" or interest on the funds over the useful life of the assets. The MRP curve is the demand schedule for capital assets at different interest rates.

Of principal concern to the utility is the future productivity or the prospective yield of the new capital investment. While it is evident that equipment will not be productive until some future date, money must be acquired and expended continuously in preparation for that point when production of the consumer product will begin. During this preparation period, interest must be paid on capital funds if new capital is to be forthcoming. This forthcoming capital is shown in Figure 2 as the marginal capital cost or supply function (MCC). To illustrate, momentarily assume that the interest rate already is determined, a machine costs $100,000, and its useful life is one year. If the capital asset in question produces a single quantity of output at year's end, and if after all expenses have been paid the net product of the machine is worth $107,000, the entrepreneuring utility finds that the particular asset has a product of $107,000 to be compared with the cost of that asset. If the

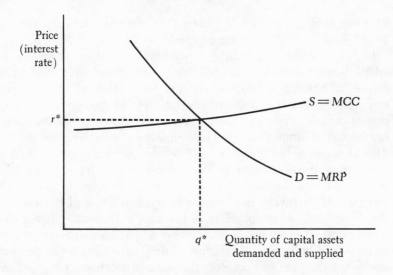

FIGURE 2. Supply of and Demand for Investment Capital

current rate of interest at the end of the year is 7 percent, that is, assuming a completely competitive money market, money is available to anyone at the 7 percent rate. From the entrepreneur's viewpoint, the investment was worthwhile as long as the return was at least 7 percent, or $7,000, which then would be available to compensate the lender for his waiting, or for that period during which he refrained from consumption. If this is exactly what was earned on the funds borrowed by the utility, the firm would consider the investment just worthwhile, or a marginal investment. The marginal revenue product or demand function (MRP) of the prospective equipment must at least equal its capital cost plus the interest rate if the asset is to be purchased or constructed.

Alternatively the firm is discounting the future yield it anticipates receiving. One might reason that the capital asset's future return one year hence of $107,000 can be discounted at the rate of 7 percent (or a present value factor of 0.934579) so that the present value is equal to its cost—$100,000. The investor wo'' 'd be willing to provide funds and the utility would be prepared to purchase new productive machinery (physical capital assets) if the value of expected future earnings, discounted to the present date, was equal to or greater than the machine's cost. A similar but more realistic analysis involves capital assets which have expected service lives of greater than one year. Similar results will be obtained for the longer time periods.

In summary, the firm desiring to purchase or construct particular capital assets must consider three factors: (1) the anticipated yield on this capital investment, determined by the summation of all anticipated earnings over the useful life of the facility; (2) the present or initial cost of the asset; and (3) the expected rate of interest or discount on investment of future earnings. The company then will have the necessary data to compare the potential yield on the physical capital assets, less the cost of these assets, with the interest and/or interest rate which must be paid on the funds borrowed from the investors to purchase the facilities. Alternatively, the firm can compare the cost of the asset with the discounted or present value of the asset's anticipated yields. With either approach a similar decision either to purchase or forego the purchase should be reached. If the net anticipated yield on the purchased assets, less the asset cost, exceeds the interest which must be paid, or if the discounted net anticipated yield exceeds the asset cost, it will be bought. Contrarily, if the interest and the original borrowing needed to repay the loan are greater than the anticipated yield, or if the cost of the new asset is greater than its discounted net anticipated yield, the asset will not be bought. The latter situation would indicate that the cost of the asset over its useful life would be greater than the anticipated returns therefrom.

It is important to remember that in deriving anticipated yields, the calculation assumes equal returns for each time period in the asset's useful life. This need not be true; the return earned during any particular period may be substantially different from other periods and at no time equal to the anticipated return. This concept is of particular importance to the public utility when the greatest portion of its costs are of a fixed nature as a result of the capital investment. Overall, one would expect that the *average* yield on the assets would be equal to those anticipated. Furthermore, one must remember that anticipated are not realized yields. If initial assumptions are incorrect, assets may earn greater or lesser amounts than assumed in the initial calculation. In the former case, the advantage will accrue to the utility; in the latter, both the investor and the utility may be losers.

Since most capital assets do not have the same life-span, one normally would expect the risk and subsequent rate of discount for longer life assets to be greater. In dealing with short- and long-lived assets, the only correct way of calculating and comparing the prospective returns therefrom is not through marginal products or anticipated yields, but through discounted marginal products or discounted anticipated yields. This procedure will produce for each asset a capital sum representing a present value of anticipated returns. Stated differently, the result will indicate the present value of the additional receipts which the utility expects to earn in the future if it employs another unit of a particular capital asset. The demand curve of these assets will slope downward to the right as does any demand curve, while their supply curve will be dictated by their price. For each such asset the supply curve will be a horizontal straight line as viewed by the individual utility, assuming that competition in the marketplace is perfect. This situation is shown in Figure 3.

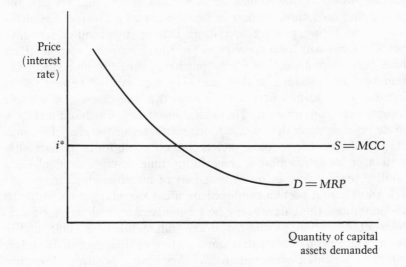

FIGURE 3.   Demand for and Supply of Investment Capital
in a Competitive Market

The utility, therefore, will increase its purchases or construction of assets until the last unit—the marginal one—has a discounted marginal revenue product (MRP) just equal to the marginal capital cost (MCC). The MCC indicates investors' willingness to supply funds. If prospective investors are to be persuaded to forego consumption and offer their money to entrepreneurs for investment in productive facilities which at some future date will provide consumable goods, then the investors must be enticed to do so. They must be offered ample reward in the form of interest sufficient to compensate them in the future for the risk which they are taking and, if necessary, for prospective returns not equaling realized returns. This is the type of reasoning necessary to justify the capitalization of allowance for funds used during construction—future compensation as a reward for waiting.

SUMMARY

As stated above, interest is the price which must be paid for the use of money capital to be converted to physical capital assets. Stated differently, it is that enticement which persuades the potential investor to allocate his disposable income between consumption and savings, and then either hold those savings in liquid form or make them available for use in future production-waiting. During any healthy economic period, groups will consume only part of their disposable income: They have two alternatives. They may purchase items for immediate consumption and pleasure, or they may choose to save all or part of the income. Thus, *savings* normally are defined as the excess of disposable income over consumption. The allocation choice which ultimately is made depends upon the relative time preference for the uses of income, that is, whether the recipient prefers to use income for immediate satisfaction or for satisfaction at some future time. Every individual has a positive time preference on at least part of his disposable income and will allocate that portion to immediate use. Depending upon particular circumstances, the balance may be accumulated in cash savings for retirement, education, purchase of a new automobile or a home, and so forth. These people prefer to retain a portion of their income for future rather than current consumption, and they have a negative rather than positive time preference on these balances.

The negative time preference is that future satisfaction or return which the saver requires on that part of disposable income which was not consumed for immediate satisfaction. While the amount of disposable income which is saved depends heavily upon the level of that income, the intensity of desire to save is also of major importance. Once the decision to save has been made, the saver must then decide to hold these savings in cash or make them available as loanable funds for the possible construction of future consumer production facilities.

When funds are made available at various interest rates, the sound economic judgment of the lender consistent with investment and interest theory is that he requires compensation commensurate with the value of his current foregone consumption. This positive time preference of foregone consumption requires that production time and therefore returns or interest must be measured from the time capital is committed to the construction of productive facilities through the time the ultimate consumer receives the finished product. This period encompasses the fabrication of both the productive facilities and the consumer good or service. As such, the economic justification for making allowance for funds used during construction is evident. When one considers the unusually long time involved in utility capital asset construction, the reward paid on this construction (allowance for funds used during construction capitalized) rightly becomes part of the cost of the capital asset, compensates the investor for waiting, and provides the incentive which assures that the waiting is worth his while.

3

Accounting Theory Underlying
Capitalization of AFC

Business enterprises can acquire tangible fixed assets in the following ways: (1) with cash; (2) through deferred payment; (3) through exchange of one noncash asset for another; (4) through exchange of their own securities; (5) through donations or discoveries; or (6) by constructing them for their own use.[1] It is from the last method that the accounting concept of capitalizing allowance for funds used during construction emanates.

Business enterprises may have different reasons for constructing assets for their own use as opposed to acquiring them by other means. Among them are: (1) Self-construction may allow the enterprise to utilize idle facilities and personnel; (2) it may afford the opportunity to effect an expected cost saving; and (3) self-construction may satisfy a need that outsiders cannot meet in the desired time.[2]

Capitalization of AFC is a controversial question in accounting

---

[1] Harry Simons, *Intermediate Accounting: Comprehensive Volume*, 5th ed. (Cincinnati: South-Western Publishing Co., 1972), pp. 433–40.

[2] Glenn A. Welsch et al., *Intermediate Accounting*, 3d ed. (Homewood, Ill.: Richard D. Irwin, 1972), p. 482.

theory. A generally accepted principle is that all charges directly attributable to a construction project should be capitalized. The disagreement arises over how to account for indirect charges. There is even greater disagreement over the handling of financing costs, that is, the interest expense incurred during a construction period. In normal circumstances, interest expense is considered to be a period financing as opposed to a period operating charge.[3] Complicating the matter even further is the question of whether interest is a cost or expense at all. Some would contend that it is not an expense of any kind, but is a specified distribution of profits.[4] Thus, the accounting literature reveals a difference of opinion as to the proper accounting for interest on borrowed funds used for construction. To add to the confusion, in the public utility industry, firms are allowed to capitalize not only the explicit interest incurred on borrowed funds, but also an implicit allowance on their own funds used for construction.[5]

In view of the controversy, the following questions merit investigation: (1) What are the underlying accounting principles which support or refute the practice of capitalizing AFC? (2) Do these principles strengthen or weaken the arguments for or against capitalizing? (3) Why is there disagreement? (4) Can the weight of accounting theory resolve the theoretical questions? (5) How has the concept itself developed historically?

Since the capitalization of AFC is an actual accounting practice, support or rejection of its use must be derived from basic accounting theory. In what follows, a theoretical discussion for capitalizing AFC will be presented. In addition, accounting principles, theories, and thought will be used to provide a structural framework which underlies the practice.

ACCOUNTING CONCEPTS AFFECTING
CAPITALIZATION OF AFC

Theories should represent foundations or frameworks upon which practices and procedures logically can be developed. This is the case with

---

[3] William W. Pyle and John Arch White, *Fundamental Accounting Principles*, 5th ed. (Homewood, Ill.: Richard D. Irwin, 1969), p. 279.

[4] Rufus Wixon et al., eds., *Accountants Handbook*, 5th ed. (New York: Ronald Press, 1965), p. 251.

[5] H. A. Finney and Herbert E. Miller, *Principles of Accounting: Intermediate*, 6th ed. (Englewood Cliffs, N.J.: Prentice-Hall, Inc., 1965), p. 295.

accounting theory, the foundation of which is postulates and concepts,[6] or what the Accounting Principles Board of the American Institute of Certified Public Accountants (AICPA) terms basic features, basic elements, and pervasive principles.[7] All of these terms have a common thread, for they form the basis of the accounting process. These propositions share the same criteria: They must serve as the foundation for the logical formulation of further propositions, and the consensus of those engaged in the accounting profession should be that they are sound or provide a starting point for the development of accounting theory.[8] The concepts used in the general theory also should be able to support specific practices.

Capitalization of AFC appears to stem from seven basic accounting concepts and from two fundamental theories. The seven concepts are the (1) business entity; (2) going concern; (3) cost; (4) revenue or income realization; (5) matching; (6) conservatism; and (7) materiality concepts. The fundamental theories are those which explain the nature of ownership equities in accounting: the proprietary and the entity theories. Each of these concepts and theories plays a part in determining whether or not AFC should be capitalized.

The Business Entity Concept

The *business entity* may be defined as "a formal or informal unit of enterprise—a collection of economic goods and services and a group of persons—organized to accomplish certain express or implied purposes. The activities of such an entity are usually oriented toward profit objectives and, in broad outline, involve the acquisition of goods and services, the transformation of these acquisitions, and the delivery of the resulting outputs to market. Accounting procedures and financial reports are

---

6 Maurice Moonitz, "The Basic Postulates of Accounting," *Accounting Research Study No. 1* (New York: AICPA, 1961), pp. 21–50; and W. A. Paton and A. C. Littleton, *An Introduction to Corporate Accounting Standards* (Iowa City: American Accounting Association, 1940), pp. 7–23.

7 APB, "Basic Concepts and Accounting Principles Underlying Financial Statements of Business Enterprises," *Statement No. 4* (New York: AICPA, October 1970), pp. 44–67.

8 Eldon S. Hendriksen, *Accounting Theory* (Homewood, Ill.: Richard D. Irwin, 1965), pp. 83–84.

concerned with specific business entities and their activities."[9] The dominant forms are sole proprietorships, partnerships, and corporations. Although the emphasis here will be upon the corporate entity, almost all conclusions can be applied to other forms as well.

The entity, a basic feature of financial accounting, collects economic goods and services by carrying on certain economic activities. These goods and services are reflected on the balance sheet as assets and are offset or balanced by the claims and equities of the entity or of those connected with it.[10]

Acceptance of the business entity concept in accounting allows for the proposition that all costs legitimately incurred by the entity properly are included in its total assets.[11] Thus, if allowance for funds used during construction is shown to be a legitimate asset cost, the entity concept may be used as support.

The Going Concern Concept

The going concern concept is an accepted convenience of both accounting and economics. It states that, in the absence of evidence to the contrary, the business enterprise assumes a continuity of existence and a presumption of stability for a period of time sufficient to carry out contemplated plans, operations, and contractual commitments.[12]

The going concern concept in accounting emphasizes valuing assets on a cost basis and on amortizing that initial cost. The idea of continuity permits the accountant to emphasize the flow of costs and to view assets as those costs awaiting ultimate amortization.[13] If AFC is a proper asset cost, then the going concern concept allows this cost to be recoverable from future revenues.

---

[9] American Accounting Association, Committee on Concepts and Standards, *Accounting and Reporting Standards for Corporate Financial Statements and Preceding Statements and Supplements* [hereafter cited as AAA, *Standards*] (Columbus, Ohio: the Association, 1957), p. 2.

[10] The entity concept should not be confused with the entity theory, which represents one of the two main ownership equity theories.

[11] Paton and Littleton, *Corporate Accounting*, p. 9.

[12] Welsch et al., *Intermediate Accounting*, p. 8.

[13] Paton and Littleton, *Corporate Accounting*, p. 11.

The Cost Concept

The cost concept is one of the most fundamental because it underlies and defines the basic subject matter of accounting. In essence, it says that cost is the proper basis of accounting for assets and expenses and that these items should be reflected in the accounts at cost as of the date of acquisition. The American Accounting Association defines the cost concept as follows: "Factors of production and other resources of an enterprise are measured at the date of acquisition by costs incurred or amounts invested on a cash or cash-equivalent basis, and at later dates by the balances of costs incurred or amounts invested after taking into account the effects of operation and other subsequent events."[14] If AFC is properly capitalized as an asset cost, its recording must be consistent with the accounting concept of cost.

The Revenue or Income Realization Concept

The normal accounting framework recognizes revenue or income when they are realized. The 1920 landmark decision in *Eisner* v. *Macomber* held that "it is the essence of income that it should be realized. . . . Income necessarily implies separation and realization. . . . The increase in the value of lands due to growth and property of the community is not income until it is realized."[15] W. A. Paton and A. C. Littleton state that "revenue is realized according to the dominant view when it is evidenced by cash receipts or receivables or other new liquid assets. Implicit here are two tests: (1) conversion through legal sale or similar process; (2) validation through the acquisition of liquid assets."[16] An America Accounting Association committee has stated that realization takes place in a revenue transaction when (1) the asset received in a revenue transaction is measurable, (2) the accounting entity is a party to a market transaction, and (3) the crucial event in the revenue process has occurred, which is the earliest time to recognize the realized revenue.[17]

---

[14] AAA, *Standards*, p. 53.

[15] *Eisner* v. *Macomber*, 25 U.S. 188, 195 (1920).

[16] Paton and Littleton, *Corporate Accounting*, p. 49.

[17] American Accounting Association, 1964 Concepts and Standards Research Study Committee, "The Realization Concept," *Accounting Review* 40 (April 1965): 314–18.

The realization concept has a bearing on the capitalization of AFC in the case of public utilities, which capitalize not only interest on borrowed funds used for construction but also an imputed allowance on other funds. In such a case, imputed interest generally is recognized as income in the period of capitalization. Theoretical questions occur as to whether capitalizing imputed interest gives rise to realized income and at what point and where the income should be recognized in the accounts. An in-depth discussion of this issue is presented in chapter 6.

The Matching Concept

Income determination in accounting is accomplished by matching costs to related revenues. Income is considered to be determined accurately if all costs relating to the earning of the revenue allocated to a current period are charged as expenses of the current period, and if all costs relating to revenue of future periods are carried forward as some kind of asset. Eldon Hendriksen gives an excellent summary of the criteria for matching costs with related revenues.

I. When costs can be reasonably associated with revenue, they should be charged to expense in the same period in which the related revenue is recognized. The following criteria may be used to establish reasonable association:

A. All costs reasonable and necessary in the production process should be classified as product costs and recorded as expenses in the period of revenue recognition.

B. When costs can be reasonably associated with specific revenue of a future period, but not with a specific product, they should be carried forward as deferred charges and matched with the related revenue when it is recognized.

II. Costs should be charged to expense in the period in which they are incurred in the following situations:

1. If there is a direct or indirect association with the revenue of the current period.

2. If there is no reasonable association with the revenue of any specific period.

3. When there is no benefit associated with any future period.[18]

---

[18] Hendriksen, *Accounting Theory*, p. 153.

There is a clear relationship between the matching concept and the question of whether or not to capitalize AFC. The matching concept determines the timing of accounting costs and expenses. Once the true nature of interest and AFC is established, the matching concept can be helpful in determining whether AFC is a charge which may be deferred.

The Conservatism Concept

The concept of conservatism in accounting is both pervasive and subtle. It arose at a time when accounting was concerned principally with the balance sheet as the major financial statement, the income statement being secondary. In the early days, accountants prepared reports mainly for bankers and other credit grantors. Since these groups were more interested in the margin of security, balance sheet conservatism was a safeguard and thus a virtue.[19] The result tended toward an understatement in assets and consequent income distortions. Later, a change in emphasis made accountants aware that balance sheet conservatism results in nonconservative income statements; thus, conservatism has become a less potent force. Today it is viewed as a moderating force falling well short of causing distortion and misrepresentation in the accounts.

The concept played an important role in the historical development of the theory of allowance for funds used during construction. As will be shown, balance sheet conservatism was used as a rationale for charging AFC as a current expense as opposed to capitalizing it. Whether this was a valid rationale merits investigation, and it will be discussed further in chapter 4.

The Materiality Concept

The concept of materiality is important in determining what financial information needs to be disclosed as opposed to that which may be ignored. The concept, in general, may be defined as follows: "A statement, fact or item is material if giving full consideration to the surrounding circumstances as they exist at the time, it is of such a nature that its disclosure, or the method of treating it, would be likely to influence or

---

[19] Finney and Miller, *Principles*, p. 143.

to 'make a difference' in the judgment and conduct of a reasonable person. The same tests apply to such words as significant, consequential, or important."[20] In 1957 the American Accounting Association defined *materiality* along very similar lines: "An item should be regarded as material if there is reason to believe that knowledge of it would influence the decisions of an informed investor."[21] Again, specific criteria were not given; thus, it appears that rational analysis of the facts available in each case must be used. Over the years, however, specific guidelines have been laid down in an attempt to help clarify the issue.[22]

The connection between the concept of materiality and allowance for funds used during construction is a general one, and the concept may help explain why the capitalization of AFC is prevalent in certain industries and yet virtually ignored in others.

BASIC EQUITY THEORIES AND THEIR IMPACT ON AFC

In defining the business entity, mention was made of the importance of not confusing the business entity concept with the entity theory. Whereas the concept defines the boundaries within which accounting information is focused, the theory represents one of the two basic explanations of how the accounting unit is perceived (the other being the proprietary theory). The proprietary and entity are the two most established and accepted theories and play an important role in the development of the rationale underlying accounting for AFC.

Both theories are an attempt to explain the nature of accounting entities. Each is very different from the other, often leading to different accounting decisions and conclusions. Also, the two theories are subjected to different perceptions and interpretations by various writers. Despite this, both represent an attempt at a theoretical conception of the true nature of the accounting entity and are necessary in establishing the proper accounting treatment of the various types of equities within the entity.

The purpose of the following sections is not to explore in detail the

---

20 James L. Dohr, "Materiality—What Does It Mean in Accounting?" *Journal of Accountancy* 90 (July 1950): 56.

21 AAA, *Standards*, p. 8.

22 See Donald Rappaport, "Materiality," *Price Waterhouse Review* 18 (Summer 1963): 26–33.

various interpretations of the two theories, but to discuss their content and relate their implications to the accounting treatment of interest and, particularly, AFC.

The Proprietary Theory

The concept of proprietorship originated historically in the attempt to complete logically the basic accounting equation. It was the notion of the proprietor which determined who was to own the assets; hence, the proprietor became the center of accounting. Thus, within the proprietary theory, the firm or business being accounted for was perceived as being owned by either a sole proprietor, a set of partners, or a group of shareholders. The assets of the firm were the property of the owners, the liabilities represented their obligations, and any excess of assets over liabilities measured the proprietorship in the business. The balance sheet equation evolved as Assets — Liabilities = Proprietorship. The business itself was a necessary convenience in accounting for assets and liabilities, but it was the proprietor who was the center of interest at all times. Under the proprietary theory, revenues were considered increases in proprietorship not resulting from investment, and expenses and losses were decreases not resulting from withdrawals of capital. Any net income resulting from operations accured directly to the proprietor.[23]

Liabilities and creditors were viewed as distinct from the proprietor. Three ways in which creditors differ from the proprietor include the following:

(1) The rights of the proprietor involve dominion over the assets and power to use them as he pleases even to alienating them; while the creditor cannot interfere with him or them except in extraordinary circumstances.

(2) The right of the creditor is limited to a definite sum which does not shrink when the assets shrink, while that of the proprietor is of an elastic value.

(3) Losses, expenses and shrinkage fall upon the proprietor alone; and profits, revenue, and increase of value benefit him alone, not his creditors.[24]

---

23 William J. Vatter, "Corporate Stock Equities," in *Modern Accounting Theory*, Morton Backer, ed. (Englewood Cliffs, N.J.: Prentice-Hall, Inc., 1966), p. 251.

24 Charles E. Sprague, *The Philosophy of Accounts* (New York: Ronald Press, 1908), p. 47.

The theory seems to be most readily adaptable to the sole proprietorship and partnership forms of organization simply because proprietorship implies personalization of ownership. It does not fit as well within the corporate framework because of the inherent legal characteristics of the organization, namely, the idea that the corporation exists apart from its owners.

The corporation being the dominant form of business organization in our economic society, attempts have been made to apply the proprietary theory within that framework.[25] Since too many inconsistencies and unanswered problems remained, writers have formulated an equity theory which they believe is more consistent with the corporate form of enterprise and also supports a logical theory of accounting. Thus, the entity theory was developed.

The Entity Theory

In the entity theory, the accounting focal point becomes the business unit or entity. The theory finds support in the legal fiction of the corporation, which stands as a separate person in its own right, and views the entity as separate and distinct from those who contribute to it. The assets and liabilities are those of the entity, not those of the shareholders or proprietors. The relation of the entity to the owners is not regarded as particularly different from that of the entity to the long-term creditors. Consequently, the balance sheet equation does not distinguish between creditors and proprietors; it reads: Assets = Equities. Any accounting of operations must be made to all the contributors of capital, not solely to the residual contributors. Paton refers to this as the managerial as opposed to the proprietary point of view.[26]

As profits are earned by the entity, they become its property and accrue to the shareholders only if a dividend is declared. Revenues and expenses also are viewed differently. Revenue represents the sales proceeds

---

25 Robert T. Sprouse, "The Significance of the Concept of the Corporation in Accounting Analyses," *Accounting Review* 32 (July 1957): 370; George R. Husband, "The Entity Concept in Accounting," *Accounting Review* 29 (October 1954): 561; Arthur N. Lorig, "Some Basic Concepts of Accounting and Their Implications," *Accounting Review* 39 (July 1964): 565; and Y. C. Chow, "The Doctrine of Proprietorship," *Accounting Review* 17 (April 1942): 162.
26 W. A. Paton, *Accounting Theory* (New York: Ronald Press, 1922), p. 52.

from the main product of the enterprise, while expenses are the consumed goods and services used in obtaining the revenue. Enterprise income results from the deduction of expense from revenue: "The entity 'accounts for' resources entrusted to it in terms of measurement of accomplishment or productivity (called revenue) and business effort (costs and expenses). The difference, *net* income, is the fundamental index of the effectiveness of the management in employing the resources entrusted to the entity and in discharging the responsibilities to equity holders. Accounting thus is income centered under the entity theory instead of being 'asset-centered' as under the proprietary theory."[27]

As in the case of the proprietary theory, different conceptions and views exist within the entity theory. There is lack of agreement regarding the appropriate perception of the firm, and confusion results as to the true nature of the equity side of the equation.[28] In any event, it appears that in more recent years the entity theory has had the greatest impact on the evolution of this body of accounting theory.

Effect of the Theories on Contractual Interest

Before any theoretical support can be established for the capitalization of AFC, the nature of contractual interest charges on debt in accounting theory should be determined.

The literature advocates two methods of viewing and handling contractual interest on obligation: as an expense or as a distribution of income. The choice of method has obvious implications for capitalizing contractual interest on funds used during construction. If interest charges are in fact distributions of income, as some believe, under no circumstances is there a basis for capitalizing such interest. On the other hand, if these charges are an expense, then one at least has passed the first step in resolving the problem, although this in itself is not sufficient.

Support for treating contractual interest charges as distributions of income comes predominantly from those who advocate the entity theory. If the enterprise is viewed as an economic entity, it makes no difference whether its resources are enhanced by bonds or stocks. In

---

[27] Welsch et al., *Intermediate Accounting*, p. 13.
[28] Stephen Gilman, *Accounting Concepts of Profit* (New York: Ronald Press, 1939), pp. 47–54; and David H. Li, "The Nature of Corporate Residual Equity under the Entity Concept," *Accounting Review* 35 (April 1960): 258–63.

either case, the entity is dealing with an investor, and there should be no fundamental difference in the treatment of return to the investor. The firm merely is using different means of raising capital. Interest payments on bonds, and dividends on stock, are distributions of corporate income.[29]

> From the point of view of the enterprise as an economic entity and a center of managerial activity, on the other hand, treatment of interest as a charge analogous to operating costs, such as labor and materials is objectionable. To management, the cost of operating the undertaking is not affected by the form of capital structure employed, nor by the particular kinds of instruments used in raising the necessary funds. To management the bondholder's dollar and the money furnished by the stockholders become amalgamated in the body of resources subject to administration, and the net income of the enterprise consists of the entire amount available for apportionment among all classes of investors. Interest charges, from this standpoint, are not operating costs but represent a distribution of income, somewhat akin to dividends.[30]

From the entity viewpoint, interest payments to bondholders are income distributions.

Another view of the entity theory seems to indicate the exact opposite. Its proponents maintain that since the corporation is a person separate and distinct from all others, any services retained by the corporation should not be so acquired without cost. Consequently, dividends, interest, and wages must be viewed as those acquisition costs.[31]

Others regard the corporation as separate from the capital-supplying group, or stockholders; consequently, capital represents the corporation's equity in itself. There are no distributions to capital suppliers, and any income belongs to the corporation and is arrived at after deducting all expenses.[32] Interest and dividends are considered expenses since there are no income distributions. From this entity theory viewpoint, interest and dividends are costs to the enterprise rather than distributions of income. This may be reasoned as follows:

---

[29] Paton, *Accounting Theory*, p. 267.
[30] Paton and Littleton, *Corporate Accounting*, pp. 43–44.
[31] Husband, "Entity Concept," p. 560.
[32] David H. Li, "Nature and Treatment of Dividends under the Entity Concept," *Accounting Review* 35 (October 1960): 675.

> To the entity then, that part of its revenue to be called income is
> the amount that can be retained, i.e., the amount it does not have
> to distribute in order to continue its existence. The primary basis
> for division of revenues from the entity's point of view is the
> urgency of distribution; whether it is a payment of wages, interest,
> or rent is not so important. On this basis prospective distributions
> of revenue may be classified as follows: (1) those due on a definite
> date and which if not made may result in legal action, (2) those
> which are scheduled for a definite date but which can be post-
> poned or eliminated without legal action on the part of the pros-
> pective recipient (interest on income bonds and dividends on
> preferred stock would be included in this category), (3) those
> which are customarily made or are expected to be made although
> not promised or legally required (dividends on common stock),
> and (4) the remainder of revenues. To which of these shall we give
> title to "income"? To an entity with the interests outlined above,
> item (4) only is income.[33]

Thus, anything prior to item four above is used to determine income
rather than represent a distribution thereof.

There appears to be much less debate as to the nature of contractual
interest on obligations under the proprietary theory. Most proponents
treat interest as an expense rather than as a distribution of income. As
previously stated, the real issue under this theory is who constitutes the
proprietors in a business corporation; the answer determines the nature
of interest. One view regards the entrepreneurs of the corporation—the
common stockholders—as the proprietors.[34] Preferred stock dividends
are classified with interest on bonds as costs.[35] "Looked at through the
eyes of the common stockholders the interest on notes, bonds, and
other liabilities would seem to be a deduction not unlike that for labor,
materials, and other operating charges. That is, from the strictly proprietary standpoint, interest represents a payment for definite service—
the use of funds furnished by bondholders and other preferential, contractual investors."[36] Others expand the proprietorship interest in the
corporation to include preferred shareholders; thus, preferred dividends

---

[33] George J. Staubus, "Payments for the Use of Capital and the Matching Process,"
    Accounting Review 27 (January 1952): 105–106.

[34] Husband, "Entity Concept," p. 561.

[35] Ibid.

[36] Paton and Littleton, *Corporate Accounting*, p. 43.

are distributions of income.[37] Bond interest, however, is still an expense. Some would include all long-term investors (including bondholders) as proprietors; therefore, interest is classified as a distribution of income along with all dividend payments.[38] The rationale is that interest on many types of debenture bonds is as subject to management discretion as common dividends, and the bondholders stand to gain or lose just as do the residual equity holders.

In summary, the question of the conceptual nature of interest in accounting theory (that is, as an expense or distribution of income) appears to be muddled and cannot be resolved by merely accepting either the proprietary or entity theory. Although the latter theory seems to offer less support for interest as an expense than does the former, there are those who use the entity theory to support the premise that interest is in fact an expense. For the purposes of this study, all contractual interest will be viewed as an expense rather than a distribution of income.

THE NATURE OF COSTS AND ASSETS

Costs in General

Having determined that there is support for treating interest as an expense, the question arises as to the appropriate accounting method for recording this item. The fact that contractual interest is deemed an expense, however, is not sufficient for stating that such interest on funds used during construction should or should not be capitalized. There are a number of additional issues to be analyzed before such a conclusion can be reached. This section will cover some of those relating to costs and interest. The discussion will revolve around costs, assets, and criteria for deferring or not deferring costs for accounting purposes. The analysis then will center on the subject of interest itself: how it is defined and how accountants view it when speaking of capitalizing allowance for funds used during construction.

Cost Defined

Cost is a word with many meanings; in economics it usually implies a sacrificing or a giving up.

---

[37] Lorig, "Basic Concepts," p. 565.
[38] Chow, "Proprietorship," p. 162.

Cost in economics means the surrender or destruction of value or the performance of some irksome activity as a means to the production of commodities or the acquisition of income. In a voluntaristic capitalist society the cost to an individual who contributes in any way to the process of production may consist of an expenditure of money, of goods for which money could be obtained, of manual or mental effort irksome at the margin; or it may involve the assumption of a physical or financial risk, the acceptance of a role carrying with it social disesteem, the choice of the less attractive of alternate ways of employing time or resources, although none of the alternatives need be of itself displeasing or irksome.[39]

The economist utilizes a very broad concept. Cost includes not only the actual costs of the services and sacrifices of laborers, capitalists, and entrepreneurs which can be measured in money terms, but also their expenditure of energy, endurance, and delaying of pleasure, which are difficult or impossible to measure. Thus, the economist also includes in the term what is commonly referred to as imputed cost.[40]

The accounting concept of cost, on the other hand, includes only the purchased commodities or the services expired of the specific business enterprise. An accounting source defines it thus: "an expenditure or outlay of cash, other property, capital stock, or services or the incurring of a liability therefor, identified with goods or services purchased or with any loss incurred, and measured in terms of the amount of cash paid or payable or the market value of other property, capital stock or services given in exchange."[41] Here costs are viewed only as goods and services rendered by outsiders to the firm and do not include any type of "implicit" or imputed cost.

The contrast lies at the heart of the present discussion because accountants sometimes tend to justify accounting theory by utilizing eco-

---

[39] Jacob Viner, "Cost," *Encyclopaedia of the Social Sciences*, vol. 4 (New York: The Macmillan Company, 1931), pp. 466–67.

[40] The Committee on Cost Concepts and Standards of the American Accounting Association defines *imputed costs* as follows: "Imputed costs are costs that do not involve at any time actual cash outlay and which do not, as a consequence, appear in the financial records; nevertheless, such costs involve a foregoing on the part of the person or persons whose costs are being calculated." See American Accounting Association, "Report of the Committee on Cost Concepts and Standards," *Accounting Review* 27 (April 1952): 178.

[41] Eric Kohler, *A Dictionary for Accountants*, 4th ed. (Englewood Cliffs, N.J.: Prentice-Hall, Inc., 1970), p. 126.

nomic principles and concepts, despite the fact that economists probably are operating within a very different framework. The issue of including imputed costs as part of accounting cost is relevant to the overall development of a theory of allowance for funds used during construction, and this subject will be expanded upon after an examination is made of the relationship in accounting of costs and assets and the criteria for capitalizing certain of these costs.

The Nature of Assets

The relationship in accounting theory between assets and costs is that the former are represented by the latter. In general, costs represent assets that await the production of future revenues. Those expired costs which are not applicable to the production of future revenues are deducted from current revenues or, on occasion, are charged against retained earnings. In attempting to develop an underlying theory of accounting for allowance for funds used during construction, however, a considerably broader analysis of the definition and nature of an asset is warranted.

John B. Canning made the first attempt to view assets as future services secured by persons or groups having legal or equitable interests in those services. "An asset is any future service in money or any future service convertible into money (except those services arising from contracts the two sides of which are proportionately unperformed) the beneficial interest in which is legally or equitably secured to some person or set of persons. Such a service is an asset only to that person or set of persons, to whom it runs."[42] This definition emphasizes the balance sheet rather than the income statement. Note that by removing the parenthetical statement the definition would appeal to a wider group than professional accountants. However, to this day accounting does not recognize as assets any contracts in which neither side has performed.

A later definition of assets illustrated a shift in emphasis from the balance sheet to the income statement: "Assets are economic resources devoted to business purposes within a specific accounting entity; they are aggregate of service-potentials available for or beneficial to expected

---

[42] John B. Canning, *The Economics of Accountancy* (New York: Ronald Press, 1929), p. 22.

operations."[43] This definition, in viewing assets as service potentials, is broader. To say simply that an asset is represented by an unexpired cost is not incorrect, but it is an oversimplification. The above definitions illustrate that an asset is more.

The following features may be attributed to assets: "(1) Inherent in assets are the positive concepts of future services, property rights, economic resources, or aggregates of service potentials. (2) Any of the above features represent assets only to those persons to whom they attach or accrue. (3) There should exist an equitable or legal claim to the rights, services, resources or service potentials that are claimed as assets."[44] These characteristics appear to be necessary and sufficient elements for the existence of assets.

Criteria for Capitalizing or Deferring Costs

Another important aspect in developing an underlying theory of accounting for AFC is to establish accounting criteria for capitalizing or deferring costs. This aspect is very closely related to the previous section because one of the distinctions between an asset (unexpired cost) and an expense (expired cost) is the issue of whether the cost is chargeable to current or future revenue. If interest is a cost (it already has been shown that it is properly viewed as an expense rather than a distribution of income), then the next logical step is to determine in particular circumstances the type of cost it represents. In order to accomplish this, it is necessary to analyze the general criteria for deferring or capitalizing costs as opposed to charging them to current revenue. One then can test to see whether interest incurred for construction of assets fits within this framework.[45]

By establishing general criteria for the capitalization or deferral of costs, the asset category is broadened beyond the usual costs represented by the tangible fixed assets to include other costs which normally might not be capitalized. In other words, costs represented by other items, such as necessary services, also properly may be deferred by meeting the required tests. There are two criteria for verifying the deferral of a cost

---

[43] AAA, *Standards*, p. 3.

[44] Hendriksen, *Accounting Theory*, p. 194.

[45] The general ideas presented below are taken from Paton and Littleton, *Corporate Accounting*, pp. 72–74.

to be applied against future revenues, and both must be met. The first test is whether or not the charge represents a legitimate cost and whether a justified expenditure has been made. The second is whether or not the charge represents an element which may benefit future periods or operations by generating future revenues. If these two criteria are met, then the cost properly may be deferred.

The above indicates there is a positive relationship between the nature of assets and the criteria for capitalizing or deferring costs. One of the stated asset characteristics is future service, which implies future benefit. Another is the existence of an equitable or legal claim. This claim most certainly would arise following the incurrence of a legitimate cost through an actual expenditure. The criteria for recognizing and recording assets or capitalized costs are essential to an understanding of whether contractual interest incurred during construction should or should not be included in the balance sheet as part of an asset's cost. This necessitates a rigorous analysis of the interest concept as an item of asset cost.

INTEREST AS A COST

It has been shown that interest on debt incurred or paid is a deduction from revenue, but no definition has been provided for *interest* as viewed by economists and accountants, and no determination has been made of its nature when used in the now superseded term "interest during construction." These issues now will be addressed.

The word *interest*, similar to the word *cost*, has a number of meanings and seems to lack a universal definition. Economists have defined *interest* both narrowly and broadly. Alfred Marshall wrote: "The payment made by a borrower for the use of a loan for, say, a year is expressed as the ratio which that payment bears to the loan." He added, however, that interest "is also used more broadly to represent the money equivalent of the whole income which is derived from capital."[46] The economist's broad meaning is derived from the fact that he views interest as a cost whose measure is the sacrifice incurred (see chapter 2).

Accountants, on the other hand, generally do not recognize as a cost any kind of interest other than that narrowly defined as contractual in-

---

[46] Marshall, *Principles*, p. 61. See also chapter 2, pp. 19–20.

terest payments due or paid on legal obligations.[47] Apparently, they are not yet ready to accept the economist's broad view. Strict adherence to accounting concepts, such as those concerning cost and revenue-income realization, prevents insertion of imputed costs and imputed interest or allowances into the financial accounts of an enterprise. At this point it might be advisable to discuss some of the factors mitigating against any general adoption of imputed costs.

Imputed costs, of which imputed interest, or allowances, on invested capital is one type, long have been considered for inclusion by accountants, but to little avail. Proponents argue that, from an economic theory viewpoint, imputed interest or allowances are as much a cost as contractual interest and should be considered in determining profits. Furthermore, this practice would provide more useful information for management in making effective business decisions, especially in regard to price-cost relationships. In 1924 Clinton Scovell argued strongly that interest on investment was merely a charge for the use of capital, and the source of capital was immaterial. Consequently, it was erroneous to include as cost the interest on borrowed money and exclude interest on owned capital.[48] In effect, this view favors the adoption of the economist's broader concept of interest.

Those who object to the inclusion of imputed costs and interest believe that there are too many problems associated with such a drastic course and that financial accounting is not a be-all and end-all for management decision. Rather, the function of financial accounting is to report the actual costs incurred by a particular enterprise, not all information which may have an influence on product-price determination.[49] Nothing prevents management from utilizing imputed costs as supplementary data, and certainly exclusion from the accounts does not preclude their use as such.

Aside from overstepping the boundaries of financial accounting, the inclusion of imputed costs and interest or allowances would undermine some of the basic concepts of financial accounting theory that were

---

[47] Note that special exceptions have been made to this general statement. For example, in the case of public utilities, accountants have allowed the recording of imputed interest in the accounts.

[48] Clinton H. Scovell, *Interest as a Cost* (New York: Ronald Press, 1924), pp. 16–18.

[49] Paton and Littleton, *Corporate Accounting*, p. 35.

discussed earlier. Two which would be violated are the cost and the revenue or income realization concepts. The former would be violated because financial accounting records only actual costs incurred. Inherent in the cost concept is the exclusion of any type of hypothetical costs, of which imputed interest represents one type. In addition, the use of imputed costs might introduce a corresponding credit to income. If these costs are attached to assets and thereby are deferred until future periods, unrealized income would be created since the offsetting credit would be admitted into income during the present period.[50] This might result in direct contradiction of the revenue or income realization principle. These are some of the cogent reasons why financial accounting has not included imputed costs in the records of account.

Even though certain financial accounting principles may be violated, the overwhelming importance of including AFC in the public utility's total asset cost base and the sound arguments of both accountants and economists justify the recognition and recording of AFC in the utility situation.

---

[50] Gilman, *Concepts of Profit*, pp. 323–24.

4

Capitalization of AFC: Historical Development

This chapter contains a chronological discussion of the relevant accounting literature dealing with the capitalization of allowance for funds used during construction and relates this literature to underlying theory.[1]

FROM THE LATE NINETEENTH CENTURY TO 1920

The literature dealing with allowance for funds used during construction dates back to the late nineteenth century. The 13 February 1886 issue of a British publication, *The Accountant*, contained an article by Edwin Guthrie, "Payment of Interest on Capital During Construction of Works."[2] This article presented some of the early legal history of

---

[1] Most of the literature tracing the historical development covering allowance for funds used during construction was written prior to 1971. As a consequence, the term accepted then, "interest during construction," was used. In order to maintain historical perspective in quotation and content, this chapter, unlike the balance of the book, will, when applicable, use that now superseded terminology.

[2] Edwin Guthrie, "Payment of Interest on Capital During Construction of Works," *Accountant* 12 (13 and 20 February 1886): 98–100 and 112–14.

interest during construction in England and a few of the basic theoretical arguments of those who supported and opposed capitalization. Guthrie attempted to present a logical argument for allowing payment of "interest" on the shareholder's capital during the period of construction. The issue arose over a standing order of Parliament which, in effect, prohibited such payments, which would have resulted in a return of capital. Guthrie maintained that passage of this order had been politically motivated rather than based upon sound economic and accounting theory. Apparently, there was no dispute in Great Britain over interest on borrowed funds; it was readily agreed that this was a true cost of construction and thus property could be capitalized. The matter of "interest" or dividends on proprietors' capital was another issue.

Guthrie and other proponents argued that there were two ways of acquiring property, by purchase or through construction. If property were acquired by purchase, interest on capital employed during the original construction of the property would be a cost to the vendor, and presumably he would include this interest in the transfer price. The means of acquiring property should not in itself have any bearing on its true value. Consequently, if property were acquired through construction and proprietors' capital were employed, any interest or dividends paid on this money should be as much a cost as if the property had been purchased. In addition, Guthrie pointed out that if borrowed money were utilized for construction and if interest were paid on these funds, there would be no objection to capitalizing that interest as part of the cost. Why then should one type of capital utilized differ from another?[3] In essence, Guthrie proposed acceptance of the economist's broad definition of costs and interest to include imputed interest. Payment of "interest" or dividends on proprietors' capital could be capitalized as costs of construction, and not considered as illegal returns of original capital.

The proponents for allowing interest to be paid out of capital won their battle with the passage of Section 91 of the Companies Consolidation Act of 1908; it became legal for companies, subject to certain restrictions which are not relevant here, to pay interest on capital during the period of construction and to capitalize this amount as part of the

---

[3] Ibid., p. 100.

cost of construction.[4] Whether the motives for passage were political or based upon the acceptance of theoretical arguments cannot readily be ascertained. Thus, for purposes of this discussion, the passage of Section 91 is not as significant as it first might appear. The fact that the law permitted payment to shareholders of "interest" or dividends during construction is not sufficient to justify the practice as sound under economic and accounting theory.

Developments in the United States followed the lead of Great Britain, but initially appeared to be more conservative. One of the early references to interest during construction was made by Henry Rand Hatfield in his 1909 edition of *Modern Accounting*. He used an example of a railroad that borrowed money to finance a road which would take several years to construct. He pointed out that, during that period, interest would have to be paid on the borrowed funds, although no revenue would be earned. Thus, these payments to bondholders were as much a cost as were materials and labor, and the road could not be constructed without incurring all of these costs. On this basis, Hatfield believed that it would be logical to capitalize this interest as part of construction costs.[5] He noted that, despite earlier opposition, the practice of including interest on borrowed funds as part of such costs had legal support in Great Britain and Germany, where even dividends paid on capital shares were legally chargeable as construction costs.[6] It appears that at this point Hatfield saw no basis in accounting for capitalizing more than interest on borrowed funds, although capitalizing dividends paid on share capital had legal sanction in certain jurisdictions.

In 1914, Arthur Lowes Dickinson wrote *Accounting Practice and Procedure*. He stated that in a going concern it was improper to charge to construction any overhead expenses which would be incurred, even if there was no construction, in which case those charges would be made against profits. However, if loans were acquired to provide funds specifically for construction purposes, or if certain other overhead charges were incurred specifically due to construction, it would be proper to charge to construction any interest on these loans. Any other approach

---

[4] Arthur Lowes Dickinson, *Accounting Practice and Procedure* (New York: Ronald Press, 1914), pp. 270–71.

[5] Henry Rand Hatfield, *Modern Accounting: Its Principles and Some of Its Problems* (New York: D. Appleton, 1909), p. 76.

[6] Ibid., p. 77.

would not be conservative and might result "in the creation of fictitious profits which could not be realized as long as the property was operated and might never be realized on its ultimate sale."[7] Dickinson did state that in constructing a new plant where no earnings were being produced it would be proper to charge any interest payments on funds borrowed for construction, as they were as necessary for completing the work as were any other costs.[8] This justification was identical to Hatfield's.

An early objection to capitalizing interest on borrowed funds was stated in a reply from the editor of the Students Department in the July 1916 issue of *Journal of Accountancy*. The question presented to the editor dealt with the propriety of charging any "interest" to construction on stock issued for that purpose. The editor responded with an unqualified "no." He went on to state his reservations as to the propriety of capitalizing any interest paid on borrowed money as a cost of construction. His reasoning was as follows:

> In spite of the consensus of opinion in favor of charging interest paid during the period of construction to the cost of a plant, it is questionable whether the practice can be defended in the last analysis. Interest is purely a cost of financiering, and its payment is a penalty for an unfortunate, although often necessary, method of providing funds for the building of a plant. It does not add anything to the intrinsic value of the plant. If it took a year to erect the plant in question and all the bond interest is to be added to its costs, say at 6%, the plant would have cost $848,000.00. If half of the cost was paid out of the capital and only the other half out of the bonds, the cost would be $824,000.00, or if the half paid for out of the bonds took only six months to build, the cost would be $812,000.00. If no bonds had been issued at all, but the capital had been made $1,200,000.00 and called up in instalments as needed to pay for the plant, there would be no interest considered, and the cost would have been $800,000.00. Therefore we have four possible values for the same plant, depending not upon any conditions connected with the plant itself, but purely upon the methods adopted to finance the undertaking.

> The question then for accountants to decide is whether it would not be better to ignore any interest cost in such a case. Of course, it would not be fair to require the profits of the first year to stand this interest charge. It should be carried as a deferred charge along

---

[7] Dickinson, *Accounting Practice*, p. 157.
[8] Ibid., p. 156.

with other expenses of organizing and starting the business and should be gradually charged off, say in five or ten years. This will be largely offset by a reduction in taxes and in depreciation caused by the lower valuation.[9]

This quote contains a basic objection to capitalizing interest on borrowed construction funds in that interest is viewed as a financing cost; consequently, it should not enter into the determination of the value of the property as it does not add to that value. The editor also questioned why a plant should have different possible values depending merely upon the modes of financing. Interestingly enough, in his 1886 article, Guthrie, in reaching the exact opposite conclusion, also reasoned that different modes of capital financing should not create different property values.[10]

FROM 1920 TO 1940

In the period prior to 1920 the literature began to discuss interest during construction. As with most beginnings, there was no deep theoretical examination of the relevant issues. However, the year 1920 marked a significant change in the pace of thought development with the publication, in the *Journal of Political Economy*, of an article by William A. Paton.[11] This was the first real attempt to apply accounting concepts and theory in answering the difficult question of whether or not interest during construction should be capitalized. The article is significant because the author sought support for his reasoning in the nature of accounting and accounting theory. For example, he stated that if construction funds are secured by a corporation through bond and stock issues, the question of how to account for interest and dividend disbursement is to be answered by adopting the view that an enterprise is an operating unit and that bondholders and stockholders as capital investors do not sell their services to the corporation. Thus, if the corporation secures funds from these investors, any disbursements

---

[9] Seymour Walton, "Interest as a Construction Cost," *Journal of Accountancy* 21 (July 1916): 68–69.

[10] Guthrie, "Payment of Interest," p. 100.

[11] William A. Paton, "Interest During Construction," *Journal of Political Economy* 28 (October 1920): 680–95.

made during the construction period would be viewed as reductions of capital, as there were no earnings at this time. Consequently, Paton concluded that it was not proper to capitalize interest during construction as a cost of construction.[12] He was a proponent of the entity concept and the entity theory of equities; hence, he based his conclusions on these underlying accounting concepts. Paton also dispelled the notion that the records of account should reflect an accrual for "interest" on investment prior to operation. He reasoned that although this "interest" represented an economic gain, it was not within the accounting framework to record it; from the viewpoint of the accounting unit, there was no real gain in any assets.[13] Paton also was one of the first to point out that, despite the impropriety of capitalizing interest during construction in the industrial enterprise, it might be perfectly logical to do so in the regulated public utility in view of the nature of the regulatory process.[14] Further discussion of this issue will be deferred to chapter 6.

Other writers have tried to use accounting theories to support or refute the capitalization practice. The construction period theory was one which seemed to lend support; its chief proponent was H. A. Finney. In his 1924 *Principles of Accounting*, Finney suggested, in essence, that all expenses incurred during a construction period may be capitalized, although after operations began these expenses properly would have been charged to revenues.[15] Bond interest was included. The main justification was that an enterprise would be spared the embarrassment of beginning operations with a deficit.[16] A similar view was stated by Charles Couchman in 1924.

> When any organization is formed, it is necessary to incur expenses before it reaches a revenue-producing condition. Apparently, this would result in an immediate deficit, unless the organization had sufficient paid-in surplus to cover it. However, it would not be good business policy to treat such costs in that way. Instead, it is an accounting fundamental quite generally recognized that a new

---

[12] Paton, "Interest," p. 694.
[13] Ibid., p. 684.
[14] Ibid., pp. 694–95.
[15] H. A. Finney, *Principles of Accounting*, vol. 2 (New York: Prentice-Hall, Inc., 1924), chapter 38, p. 12.
[16] Ibid.

organization need not report a deficit during its process of forma-
tion. Instead, all costs necessary to bring the business to a revenue-
producing stage may properly be capitalized, that is treated as
assets, to be written off as expense during a reasonable time if
desired.[17]

The principle of avoiding embarrassment is not a very effective argument. The idea that a business should not start operations with a deficit
is unsound; there is nothing inviolate about the period prior to operations which should preclude the possibility of incurring a loss at that
time.[18]

D. R. Scott, in his 1925 book, *Theory of Accounts*, saw the concept
of objective evidence as a guideline to be used in determining whether
or not interest paid on borrowed funds during construction is properly
charged to the asset. "If the construction is carried on under a competitive contract which covers the matter of time allowed for it, all interest paid upon funds borrowed to finance the construction may be
charged to the value of the completed assets. If, however, a firm does its
own construction, the case with respect to interest paid is not so clear.
The rate of interest paid will be competitively determined but not the
total amount since the length of the construction period is not so determined."[19] Although Scott believed that custom ruled against charging
to assets any amount for the income foregone by the stockholders during
the period of construction, he saw no objection to allowing such a
charge at the long-term borrowing rate upon loans, provided that an
offsetting credit were made to a reserve account. Scott believed that, by
permitting this practice, depreciation taken would represent the recovery of whole costs.[20] The latent weakness in this proposition is that, at
best, whole cost can be recovered only when the long-term borrowing
rate is equal to the opportunity cost of stockholder investment. Apparently this weakness prevented Scott's proposal from receiving further
support in the literature.

The 1930s witnessed a strong interest in the topic of interest during
construction. The major portion of the relevant literature consisted of

---

[17] Charles B. Couchman, *The Balance Sheet: Its Preparation, Content, and Interpretation* (New York: The Journal of Accountancy, Inc., 1924), p. 145.

[18] Paton, *Accounting Theory*, p. 287.

[19] D. R. Scott, *Theory of Accounts*, vol. 1 (New York: Henry Holt, 1925), p. 265.

[20] Ibid., pp. 95–96.

correspondence to and replies from the American Institute of Accountants, published in the *Journal of Accountancy*. Apparently, little head-
way was made in establishing an underlying theory. Rather, the literature reflects the many diverse opinions held by the accounting profession
on this subject. From among this correspondence, three basic questions
were submitted to the *Journal* which have theoretical relevance for our
discussion.

The first, which appeared in the May 1930 issue,[21] involved an industrial subsidiary that acquired construction funds from (1) sale of interest-
bearing obligations, (2) sale of capital stock, and (3) retained earnings.
The question dealt with the type of interest to be properly capitalized
during construction. The first reply stated that, in a going business, for
reasons of conservatism, it usually was considered preferable not to
capitalize any interest. The reply added, however, that there was nothing
wrong with capitalizing interest on any of these funds, regardless of their
source. Furthermore, any interest capitalized on the company's own
funds could be included as part of current income. The response of a
second correspondent was substantially different. He pointed out that,
in dealing with business enterprises other than public utilities, any interest capitalized during construction should be limited to interest actually
paid on borrowed funds used for construction purposes. The only interest which properly could be charged as a cost of construction would
be that paid on the interest-bearing obligations. He did add that if a
contrary view were taken, and if interest on the company's own funds
were capitalized, then the credit should not go to income, but to capital
surplus. The answer given by a third correspondent was similar to that
of the first. He believed that interest actually paid on borrowed funds
usually was considered a proper cost of construction, but that conservative practice would not sanction capitalizing interest on a company's
own funds. This correspondent believed, as did the first, that such a
practice was not improper if clearly disclosed in the published accounts.

In analyzing these answers several points should be noted. None of
the three seem to be based upon sound underlying theory, nor is any
attempt made to support the answers with theoretical concepts, other
than the concept of conservatism. A possible explanation might be that

---

[21] Accounting Questions, "Interest on Construction Cost," *Journal of Accountancy*
49 (May 1930): 388–90.

the question represented a real-world problem; thus, the answers were given in terms of how actual accounting practice would handle it. This also might explain why two of the correspondents, who presumably were accountants, would sanction the capitalization of interest on other than borrowed funds used for construction when up to this time there had been little or no theoretical support for this practice in the literature. Thus, there appears to have been some gap between theory and practice.

In the June 1932 issue of the *Journal of Accountancy* another relevant question appeared.[22] The case involved the treatment of interest payable on certain notes issued to finance construction of a hotel. The question was whether, under accounting principles, the party constructing the hotel had to capitalize the interest paid during the construction period, or could the interest be considered merely discretionary and thus expensed. The questioner wanted to expense the interest to reduce the tax liability of the corporation, which was in receivership, apparently under the mistaken belief that if the interest was capitalized for accounting purposes, the same would have to be done for tax purposes, thus possibly losing the interest deduction. The three answers given to this question were similar in their conclusions that, from an accounting standpoint, it is best to capitalize interest paid during construction rather than to expense it. What is interesting about the answers is not their conclusions, but the reasoning used to support them. The general reasons were: (1) Accounting theory supported this treatment in works of well-known authors; (2) capitalization of interest during construction was prescribed for public utilities under their various uniform systems of accounts; and (3) interest should have been capitalized because it was not good practice to show a loss during the construction period by reason of the mode of financing.

Although it is difficult to dispute the first reason because of its generality and lack of controversy, exception is taken to the other two. The fact that most public utilities capitalize interest during construction under their respective uniform systems of accounts does not in any way represent a justification in accounting for commercial enterprises to do the same; the nature of the regulatory environment in which utilities

---

22 Accounting Questions, "Interest Payable During Construction," *Journal of Accountancy* 53 (June 1932): 473–75.

operate makes comparison impossible. As to the third reason, the point was made previously that capitalizing any cost merely to avoid the embarrassment of beginning operations with a deficit is not a sound or effective argument to be used in justifying the practice.[23]

By the late 1930s, a glimmer of progress appeared in response to a question in the August 1938 issue of the *Journal of Accountancy* dealing with the propriety of capitalizing preferred dividends paid during construction.[24] The particulars of the case involved an industrial corporation which was formed for the purpose of building and running a mill. Bonds and preferred and common stocks were sold to finance the construction, the common stock being sold at 33⅓ percent premium, the premium being available for the payment of preferred dividends during the period of construction. During that period preferred dividends were declared and paid out of surplus. The questions asked whether these payments could be capitalized in order to conserve the paid-in surplus for future contingencies, and whether there was any authority which would defend such a practice. As before, the relevance of this case to the present discussion lies in the answers given.

The first correspondent cited what he believed to be an analogous situation dealing with income bonds found in Robert H. Montgomery's *Auditing Theory and Practice*. Montgomery believed that, when income bonds were outstanding during a period of construction and it was expected that interest would be paid, it was proper to capitalize the interest even though payment depended upon sufficient income and upon authorization of payment by the directors. The correspondent's opinion was that if it were permissible to capitalize interest on these income bonds, then certainly it was permissible to capitalize dividends actually paid on preferred stock out of paid-in surplus. The analogy appears to be a poor one because of the intrinsic difference between interest on income bonds as representing costs, and dividends on preferred stock as representing distributions of income. The correspondent's answer seems to infer that it is proper to capitalize dividends paid on preferred stock simply because they had been paid. He failed, however, to observe the distinct possibility that preferred dividends simply are not analogous to interest on any type of debt obligation. The response

---

[23] See p. 55.

[24] Accounting Questions, "Dividends Paid During Construction," *Journal of Accountancy* 66 (August 1938): 117–19.

of the second correspondent also illustrates an inherent weakness. He stated that, although not in the case of the normal industrial enterprise, in the unique instance of a regulated utility all elements of cost should be included in the property accounts, or these costs might never be recovered. For this reason, interest during construction was not capitalized in all cases. He concluded, apparently because a public utility was not involved in the case in question, the preferable treatment would have been to capitalize only the actual interest cost paid and to charge the dividends paid on the preferred stock to paid-in surplus. Once again, the consistency or logic of the argument is unclear. A theoretical support for accounting practice should be based upon concepts and principles and should not be based on the particular type of industry involved with the problem.

It was in the answer of a third correspondent that an attempt was made to use some underlying accounting principles and concepts. His opinion was that, under accepted accounting practice, it is not proper to capitalize preferred dividends paid during construction. His reasoning was based on the fact that, under normal circumstances, a payment of preferred dividends is a distribution of earnings and not a cost of any kind. Thus, if no present or accumulated earnings are available, and if preferred dividends are paid out of paid-in surplus, such a dividend is a return of capital, and under no circumstances should such a payment be charged to an asset account. Capitalizing dividends paid in an attempt to conserve paid-in surplus for future contingencies would represent a clear misstatement of the accounts.

FROM 1940 TO 1960

The period 1940–1960 was essentially one when renowned accounting authors discussed interest during construction in textbooks and periodicals. Some of these authors, such as Finney and Paton, who previously had written about interest during construction, either had expanded or, as in Paton's case, changed their views. Also, commencing with the 1950s, a new emphasis appeared. Prior to this period, writers made only passing references to the fact that public utilities actively capitalized interest during construction and that it was sanctioned under their respective uniform systems of accounts, but in the 1950s the preponderance of the literature dealt with accounting for such interest in the public utilities industry. In this study, however, all major discussion of accounting for interest during construction in public utilities will be deferred until chapter 6.

In his 1941 *General Accounting*, Finney wrote that although, of necessity, regulatory commissions permitted utilities to capitalize interest paid during construction in the cost of fixed assets in order to allow their recovery, he could see no reason for allowing industrial companies to do so, despite the fact that it was done. Finney believed that interest paid on debt by any type of enterprise, regulated or unregulated, was not a necessary cost of construction because this type of financing could be avoided by the use of equity funds. He further believed that, since interest paid on borrowed funds was not a necessary cost of construction, this accounting practice was illogical because the value of an asset should not be enhanced when one type of financing is used in place of another.[25] Finney believed the practice had become so well entrenched in the unregulated sector that it was rarely challenged, despite its inherent lack of logic.

An apparent weakness exists in Finney's reasoning that interest on borrowed funds is not a necessary cost of construction. He seems to overlook the importance of a balanced capitalization structure for any corporate enterprise. For example, Graham and Dodd state that it is necessary for any industrial company (including a public utility) of any size and reasonable stability to have reasonable amounts of debt as part of its capital structure.[26] If this is the case, then debt is necessary. If interest is an accounting cost, it may be a necessary cost of construction if utilized for that purpose. Thus, it is very unlikely that a company can avoid using some of its borrowed funds in constructing facilities if the firm has a reasonable component of debt in its capital structure and also utilizes large amounts of funds for construction. For these reasons, Finney's statement, that interest paid during construction is not a necessary cost, lacks support.

Whereas Finney seemed to expand his views on the subject during this period, Paton, in his 1952 *Asset Accounting*, radically altered his earlier opinions. Paton previously had stated that interest on borrowed funds and preferred dividends are, under the entity theory, distributions

---

[25] H. A. Finney, *General Accounting* (New York: Prentice-Hall, Inc., 1941), p. 259.
[26] Benjamin Graham, David L. Dodd et al., *Security Analysis, Principles and Technique*, 4th ed. (New York: McGraw-Hill, 1962), p. 549.

of capital.[27] At that time, he strongly believed that the entity theory was the most meaningful in accounting for corporate activities; consequently, he based his conclusions upon it. By 1952 Paton apparently had come to believe that, for purposes of accounting for interest during construction, the corporation, although a separate entity, had to be viewed not by itself, but through the eyes of some group or interest. The common stockholders or, as he phrased it, the "residual equityholders,"[28] were most representative of the corporate membership and had the most authority. The shift toward a proprietary or residual equity view of the corporate entity meant that Paton also viewed interest and preferred dividends differently. From the common stockholders' viewpoint, interest paid during construction was not a return to a group of capital suppliers, but represented a service furnished and sold by the creditors to the common stockholders. Rather than a reduction in the stockholder's investment, this interest was a real cost incurred, on a sound commercial basis, to the advantage of the stockholder. Thus, there was no reduction in any corporate resources because of interest paid during construction.[29]

Continuing this line of reasoning, Paton discussed alternative ways of assigning this interest to the asset accounts. One option, supported by some, but opposed by Paton, is to assign it to the individual assets acquired in terms of the respective amounts of funds employed. Paton disagreed, believing that this would mean all assets, including liquid resources such as cash used during construction, also should be assignsed a carrying charge if they were acquired with the borrowed funds. Paton's opinion was that the mode of financing a particular asset should not affect the cost of that asset. Instead, any interest during construction should be viewed as a general financing cost incurred to get the business operating and therefore should be charged to a special account rather than to each of the individual asset accounts. This interest cost then would become a permanent asset, similar to organization costs, and not subject to amortization. Paton also thought that viewing interest during construction as similar to organization costs would in no way preclude the possibility of capitalizing interest during construction on capital

[27] See p. 40.
[28] William A. Paton and William A. Paton, Jr., *Asset Accounting* (New York: Macmillan, 1952), p. 475.
[29] Ibid.

additions to the entity after its initial launching; these additions would be considered new operations, and interest charges thus properly could be capitalized.

Consistent with his shift in emphasis from the entity to the residual equity point of view, Paton came to regard preferred stocks, similar to bonds, as senior securities; as is the case with interest on borrowed funds, any preferred dividends paid during construction also are financing costs incurred on a sound commercial basis, not returns of capital. To support this proposition, in 1952 Paton asserted that preferred stocks are more nearly related to debt securities than to the residual common equity, as evidenced by the fact that, in some cases, preferred stocks have set dividend requirements similar to the coupon rate on bonds. In addition, preferred issues often are callable and have gradual retirement through sinking fund provisions.[30] Paton concluded that preferred dividends paid during construction are very similar to interest on borrowed funds, and it is therefore equally logical to capitalize them. Regarding capitalization of any imputed cost of funds provided by the residual equity, Paton held to the same view stated in his 1920 article that "interest" on investment should not be accrued on the books of account.[31]

FROM 1960 TO THE PRESENT

As in the 1950s, much of the recent literature on interest during construction emphasizes practical problems in accounting for interest during construction. With respect to resolving the theoretical issues, the limited material written on the subject during the 1960s contributes little new insight, and attempts at developing a theoretical basis resemble those made in previous periods. For example, the *Journal of Accountancy* received an inquiry in October 1960 from an insurance executive regarding the propriety of capitalizing interest on borrowed funds used for construction of an office building. Carman Blough, then director of research for the AICPA, was of the opinion that, although the practice was not prevalent outside the public utility field, in theory there was equal justification for capitalizing such interest in the unregulated in-

---

[30] Ibid., p. 476.
[31] See pp. 53–54.

dustries.[32] He reasoned that interest is not an operating expense, but is a cost of preparing the asset for operations. He added that it is unreasonable for a new business, which must borrow funds for construction purposes, to be forced into showing a loss before operations begin because it could not capitalize the interest on those funds. Blough's first reason is merely a restatement of Finney's construction period theory, which stated that all expenditures incurred for the purpose of construction properly are included in asset cost. His second reason represents one of the underlying justifications in support of Finney's theory, a justification which previously was shown to be unsound.[33]

The sixth edition of *Principles of Intermediate Accounting* by Finney and H. E. Miller expands somewhat on the views expressed by Finney in 1941 with regard to the capitalization of interest on borrowed funds used for construction by an unregulated company.[34] The 1965 edition states the following:

> The issue concerning the propriety of capitalizing interest in the case of non-regulated companies generally arises during the "start-up" period when the new business has construction activity but little, if any, revenue. During such a period, capitalization has some theoretical appeal because it can lead to a better matching of revenue and expense. However, assuming that justification is found to support the capitalization of interest during an organization period, it would be better if the amount were charged to an intangible asset rather than to a tangible asset as part of its cost.[35]

There are a number of significant points in this statement. First, the matching concept is offered as possible theoretical support for capitalizing interest during construction during a start-up period. If interest is incurred during a construction period, it is best to defer that cost until it can be matched with the future earnings of the asset being constructed. The matching concept alone, however, did not seem to influence the author's general opposition to capitalization. Second, Finney

---

[32] Carman G. Blough, ed., "Capitalization of Interest During Construction," *Journal of Accountancy* 110 (October 1960): 80.

[33] See p. 55.

[34] Finney and Miller, *Principles*, pp. 295–96. See p. xx.

[35] Finney and Miller, *Principles*, p. 296.

and Miller appear to agree with Paton that, during a start-up period,[36] interest during construction is in the nature of an organizational cost and thus should not be charged to specific tangible assets.

In conclusion, it is of value to mention Harold Bierman's attempt in 1965 to revive the argument that accounts should recognize imputed interest.[37] Bierman argues that, unless interest during construction is capitalized (including implicit interest on equity capital), assets and net income of early periods will be understated, and net income of later periods will be overstated. To nullify the argument that capitalizing imputed interest will create profits on construction, Bierman suggests that an unrealized income account be credited to stockholder's equity and the credits be recognized in the income statement as the asset constructed is depreciated. Thus, once again, the interest during construction issue raises the more general question of introducing imputed costs into the books of account. As previously discussed, however, the present framework of accepted accounting concepts probably will not support such recognition of imputed costs.[38]

---

[36] For purposes of this discussion, the term "start-up period" is applicable not only to a new business, but also to a going concern which constructs capital additions to increase its size. In this circumstance the additions can be viewed as new operations.

[37] Harold Bierman, *Financial Accounting Theory* (New York: Macmillan, 1965), pp. 58–60.

[38] See above page 47.

5

Procedures for Determining
AFC in the Electric Utility Industry

The fact that rates are regulated in the electric utility industry is one of the key factors distinguishing it from ordinary commercial or industrial enterprises. In the regulated utility situation, investors are limited by law to a fair return on investment, which is consistent with the concept of a utility's revenue requirements being equal to its "cost of service."[1] When a stockholder invests his capital in an industrial or commercial enterprise, he does so with the knowledge that the company's return will not be limited by direct government regulation. Consequently, when construction is undertaken which delays any immediate return, the stockholder is aware that he still can be compensated in the future for his loss of income during the construction period, depending only upon the profit-making capacity of the firm. In the utility enterprise, however, due to the presence of regulation, this is not the case. Unless special provision is made for an investor to earn a return during a construction period, he may suffer a loss which may never be recovered in the future. Certainly no investor would provide an enterprise with capital during a period when no earnings were present unless he knew that eventually he would be compensated in some way. Since, under

---

[1] Paul J. Garfield and Wallace P. Lovejoy, *Public Utility Economics* (Englewood Cliffs, N.J.: Prentice-Hall, 1964), p. 44.

utility regulation, it is the general practice to keep plant construction costs out of the rate base until that plant becomes part of the utility's "used and useful" property, the utility recovers this cost from its customers by recording it in the plant accounts so that eventually it can be included in the rate base.[2] Capitalizing allowance for funds used during construction is the means through which these costs eventually can be recovered.

The uniform systems of accounts sanction the inclusion of AFC as a component of construction cost, thus permitting a utility to recover capital costs by capitalizing an amount representing the cost of both borrowed funds and other funds used for construction. By allowing the capitalization of these other funds, the unique situation is created within the regulatory process whereby a certain *imputed* amount is recognized in the records of account. This is contrary to the existing practice among unregulated enterprises, in which area, for various reasons, the inclusion of imputed costs in the records of account traditionally has been rejected.[3] The question then arises as to whether these traditional objections should apply. as well to public utility accounting, or whether the circumstance of regulation in the utility situation somehow overrides these objections. This is not meant to imply that public utility accounting need not adhere to basically the same scheme of accounting as any other enterprise; however, at times the nature of regulation may require certain departures from procedures normally used in the unregulated situation. The burden still rests upon the utilities and the regulators to justify their practices as sound and necessary.

CAPITALIZING AFC: EXTENT OF USE

The practice of capitalizing AFC has been the device most frequently used by electric utilities to recover capital costs incurred in financing construction.[4] The extent of this practice can be gauged by the results of annual surveys conducted by Duff and Phelps, Inc. Surveys made from 1968 through 1971 are displayed in Table 3 and show the number

---

2 James C. Bonbright, *Principles of Public Utility Rates* (New York: Columbia University Press, 1961), p. 178.

3 See chapter 3, p. 47, and footnotes 48 through 50.

4 Although alternative means other than capitalizing AFC do exist for recovery of capital costs, these have received only limited use. A discussion of these alternatives together with advantages and disadvantages will be given in chapter 7.

TABLE 3. Interest during Construction Survey by Duff and Phelps, Inc., 1968–1971

Types of utility	March 1968		May 1969		April 1970		May 1971	
	Polled	Replies	Polled	Replies	Polled	Replies	Polled	Replies
Electric and predominantly electric	109	103	109	109	109	108	109	108
Utilities capitalizing interest during construction		98		106		104		105
Utilities not capitalizing interest during construction		5		3		4		3
Total		103		109		108		108

Source: Duff and Phelps, Inc., *Interest During Construction Survey* (March 1968, May 1969, April 1970, May 1971).

of electric utilities capitalizing AFC during that time.[5] The conclusion is that the overwhelming majority of electric companies do follow the capitalization practice. Neither the more recent 1973 poll[6] nor the 1970 questionnaire mailed in connection with this study showed any change in this situation.[7] The questionnaire responses revealed that of 130 Class A and B electric utilities,[8] 125 reported capitalizing AFC.

CAPITALIZING AFC: METHODS AND PRACTICES

Although capitalizing AFC as an element of plant cost is widely recognized and used by most electric companies, there are many variations in policies and methods used in determining what and how much is capitalized. To date, the overall development of sound and practical methods have been left primarily to the discretion of individual utilities, subject only to specific decisions and pronouncements of regulatory commissions having jurisdiction.

Under the uniform systems of accounts, utilities are required to record all costs incurred in the construction of utility plants by means of work or job orders. A work order system is designed to show (1) the nature of each addition of plant constructed, (2) the total costs of construction, (3) the sources of the costs, and (4) the plant accounts to be charged or credited.[9] Work orders may be issued for specific projects or as blanket or standing orders. The latter cover all plant jobs of a certain class during a given year, such as line transformer changes, electric service installations, or other distribution plant work. The work or job order system provides, in convenient form, all the costs of specific construction work and thus permits a ready analysis of such utility expenditures. AFC as a component of construction cost enters the accounting records through the work order system; likewise, the work order provides certain basic information for determining the amount of AFC to be capitalized.

---

[5] Duff and Phelps, Inc., *Interest During Construction Survey* (New York: March 1968, May 1969, April 1970, May 1971).

[6] Duff and Phelps, Inc., *Allowance Used for Funds Survey* (New York: July 1973).

[7] See Appendix B for selected information in questionnaire survey.

[8] Class A utilities are those having annual electric operating revenues of $2.5 million or more. Class B utilities are those with annual electric operating revenues of $1 million or more but less than $2.5 million.

[9] FPC, *Uniform System*, pp. 101–14, as amended

The majority of electric utilities determine capitalized AFC by applying a particular capitalization rate to a base composed of construction expenditure balances accumulated from work orders. Thus, three main elements which must be considered are (1) the interest capitalization rate, (2) the base to which this rate is applied, and (3) the time period. The proper treatment of these elements has been the subject of disagreement both among the utilities and between the utilities and regulatory authorities. Each element will be discussed below in terms of how it has been used in determining capitalized AFC and the problems faced by the electric utilities in applying these elements.

The ensuing treatment of methods and practices will be based in large part on an analysis of responses received through the mail questionnaire mentioned previously. Those results and rate-case decisions of regulatory commissions regarding the factors used in determining the amounts of capitalized AFC are analyzed in topical sequence in the remaining sections of this chapter.[10]

The questionnaire aided in providing the following basic information regarding individual company practices: (1) the base and methods used in calculating AFC and variations or modifications to the base, including determination of the dollar expenditure base and items of property excluded from it; (2) whether or not AFC is compounded; (3) properties and jobs not subject to AFC capitalized, with specific reference to the nondepreciable asset, land; (4) minimum dollar amounts and time periods below which AFC is not calculated; (5) the time period during which AFC is capitalized; and (6) the capitalization rates used in calculating AFC and the basis for determining these rates.

Capitalizing AFC: Determining the Base

Two general bases used by electric utilities in computing the dollar amounts of AFC capitalized are the funds available and funds expended bases. The former requires that specific funds be earmarked and segregated in financing construction projects. Interest is accrued and capitalized from the time the funds are available until the project is completed. Due to inherent difficulties associated with this method, that is, specific types of funds easily cannot be identified with expenditures for

---

[10] A copy of the entire questionnaire and a distribution of the individual responses are reproduced in Appendixes A and B.

construction activities, it presently is used by very few utilities. In fact, the questionnaire revealed that none of the electric utilities reported using the funds available basis.

THE DOLLAR EXPENDITURE BASE. The funds expended basis apparently is the predominant method used by utilities in determining the dollar amounts of capitalized AFC. Utilities apply a capitalization rate to a base composed of a balance of certain construction expenditures incurred during the period of construction. Subject to minor variations, virtually all utilities responding to the questionnaire used one of the following three time period methods in determining a base: (A) month ending balances; (B) average of month's beginning and ending balances; or (C) month beginning balance plus one-half the current month's expenditures.

The example in Exhibit 2 illustrates how each of these methods is applied in determining the base. Note that methods B and C always will yield the same result.[11] The implicit, underlying assumption of these methods is that expenditures are evenly distributed over the month, a more tenable assumption than is made for method A, which uses a month ending balance figure. Interestingly enough, method A will yield the same total base as the other two when only one-half the final month's expenditure is used. However, if method A uses one-half the final month's expenditure, since the amount of AFC capitalized normally is determined monthly to avoid large credits to income at the project's close, individual monthly amounts will not be the same as under methods B and C, even if it is assumed that similar rates and construction periods are involved in the computations.

The method most appropriate for a given utility depends upon how the firm *actually* incurs its monthly construction expenditures or upon how these are assumed to be incurred. Method A would be preferable if all monthly construction expenditures were incurred at the beginning of the month. When expenditures are distributed over the entire month, which is probably more common, methods B or C would be more appropriate.

Actual use of these methods by electric utilities can be evaluated from Table 4, which presents a frequency distribution of the responses to item

---

[11] Let $x =$ month beginning balance, and $y =$ month ending balance:

Method B: $\dfrac{x+y}{2}$;　　　Method C: $x + \dfrac{(y-x)}{2} = \dfrac{x+y}{2}$

EXHIBIT 2. Methods Used to Determine Base for Capitalizing AFC, Funds Expended Basis

Month of construction	Monthly expenditures excluding prior AFC	Accumulated balance at month's end
June 30	$00,000	$00,000
July 31	30,000	30,000
August 31	15,000	45,000
September 30	25,000	70,000
October 20	10,000	80,000
	$80,000	

Computation of base in	Method A, month ending balance	Method B, average of month's beginning and ending balances	Method C, month beginning balance plus one-half current month's expenditures
August for July	$ 30,000	$ 15,000	$ 15,000
September for August	45,000	37,500	37,500
October for September	70,000	57,500	57,500
November for October	80,000	75,000	75,000

Assumptions:
(1) Job authorized: $80,000
(2) Start of construction: 1 July 1975
(3) Plant put in service: 21 October 1975

five of the questionnaire. Table 4 indicates that the number of firms using method A (Code 1) is approximately equal to those using methods B and C combined (Codes 3 and 4). Only two utilities reported adjusting method A by taking one-half the final month's expenditures (Code 2).

TABLE 4.   Methods Used in Base Determination Reported in the Survey

Description of method	Code	Number of companies	Responses (percentage)
Other	0	6	4.6
Prior month ending balance, method A	1	47	36.2
Prior month ending balance, one-half expenditures in final month	2	2	1.5
Average of month's beginning and ending balance, method B	3	10	7.7
Month beginning balance plus one-half current month's expenditure, method C	4	36	27.7
Inappropriate	8	5	3.8
Not ascertained	9	24	18.5
Total		130	100.0

The funds expended computation basis methods are applied with some time period variation by a number of the respondents. For example, some utilities assume that construction jobs of a certain dollar range, on the average, are operative at the middle of the last month of construction; consequently, capitalized AFC is computed for one-half the final month. Others capitalize AFC in the last month if construction is completed in the first half of the month. A number of utilities that use electronic data processing equipment to determine the amount of AFC capitalized reported facilitating the process by assuming that the first and last months of construction projects are half months. For very large construction projects, such as fossil and nuclear fuel plants, which involve substantial amounts of capitalized AFC, many utilities calculate the final month's amount based on actual days prior to the in-service date. This practice assures that no significant amounts of capitalized AFC are lost due to the failure to consider the entire construction period; it also prevents an overaccrual in the final month. When less significant amounts are involved, many utilities reported that they capitalize AFC only once, at the project's completion, basing the computation on total expenditures.

For the most part, the regulatory commissions apparently have left the choice of method to the individual utilities. In only three instances has the Federal Power Commission suggested a specific capitalization basis. In these cases the FPC suggested that the allowance be computed monthly "on the accumulated total of net approved project costs, other than interest, as of the first day of each month; plus one half of the net approved project costs, other than interest, for the month of computation."[12] One questionnaire respondent whose firm uses method C noted that this method was suggested by the FPC. Available evidence thus seems to indicate that the FPC favors that method.

PROPERTY EXCLUDED. In determining the total dollar amount under the funds expended basis, utilities reported that certain items often are deducted from the expenditure base. Among the items in this category are: (1) contract retentions; (2) advances to contractors for construction; (3) unpaid liabilities (accruals); (4) capitalized property taxes; (5) apportioned overhead, such as administrative and general expenses; and (6) prior interest capitalized.

With regard to item five, some firms reported that they exclude all overheads in the base, while others include only direct job overheads because general apportioned overheads are applied only at completion of the projects. At least five utilities reported that they include all such, including general overheads, in determining the expenditure base. The test for inclusion or exclusion of general overheads apparently rests upon whether these items are allocated periodically during construction or only once at the completion of the project.

Compounding AFC Capitalized

Of the utilities that reported capitalizing AFC, only four reported that they, at one time or another, compounded the allowance, that is, left prior AFC capitalized in the expenditure base in computing the current portion. Another four were considering using the practice, while thirteen others were not sure of their future plans. Although there may be theoretical justification for compounding, a number of practical

---

[12] Re Inland Power and Light Co. (1942) 3 FPC 321; Alabama Power Co. (1941) 2 FPC 443; and Minnesota Power and Light Co. (1948) 7 FPC 102.

reasons have tended to preclude its widespread adoption.

Theoretically, one may argue that the actual interest costs on borrowed funds and those imputed on other funds are as much components of construction costs as are other overheads that are properly capitalized and included in the base upon which any future allowances are capitalized. It would seem to follow that "interest" itself also should be included so that the utility can be compensated for the time that these funds are tied up in construction and not yet in the rate base. Despite this apparent justification, the practice has not gained broad acceptance. First, the present methods used in calculating the dollar amounts of AFC capitalized are, of necessity, merely estimates. There appears to be very little effort on the part of utilities to isolate or evaluate precisely each of the elements involved. Second, a review of FPC decisions reveals that the commission consistently has disallowed compounding AFC.[13] With this in mind, utilities apparently decided that the issue is not sufficiently important to challenge on theoretical grounds and thus tacitly have accepted the commission's refusal to allow compounding in the base. With construction work relatively less important and with inflation at a minimum in the past, these approaches to compounding AFC probably had minimal effect on construction costs.

However, under today's conditions of ever increasing construction programs the compounding question becomes more relevant. This is evident in a recent technical release by the New York Public Service Commission. The release, taking effect at date of issue, resulted from the commission's consideration of the compounding issue in a Long Island Lighting Company case where the commission stated:

> Lastly, we conclude that the policy of not calculating IDC on that portion of construction work in progress represented by past IDC accruals should be reevaluated. In fact, utilities do incur additional capital costs on accrued IDC. In the past, when interest rates were lower, construction budgets smaller and construction periods shorter, the cost of financing accrued IDC may have been minimal. At present, this is not the case. LILCO's test year average IDC approximated $13.5 million; carrying charges on this total would have been more than $1 million. We conclude that it is no longer

---

[13] *Chelan Electric Co.* (1933) 1 FPC 99, 110; *Alabama Power Co.* (1941) 2 FPC 443; *Re Lexington Water Power Co.* (1937) 1 FPC 438; and *Re Inland Power and Light Co.* (1942) 3 FPC 321.

proper to continue an accounting practice which, in effect, ignores what is now a substantial element of construction costs. Accordingly, LILCO may revise its accounting practices so that in the future IDC will be taken on the entire balance of interest bearing construction work in progress, including accrued interest. This change, if made, will be entirely prospective in nature and will have no impact on the rates approved in this proceeding.[14]

Although the above was directed specifically to Long Island Lighting Company, the accounting release authorized similar revision in accounting for AFC by New York Class A and B electric utilities effective with interest capitalized in January 1975.[15]

Properties and Jobs Not Subject to AFC

Theoretically, the purpose of capitalizing AFC is to allow utilities to recover the capital costs of, and to earn a return on, funds devoted to construction. If this is an acceptable premise, then utilities should capitalize AFC on all construction expenditures, irrespective of the amount, time period, or type of property involved. Many electric utilities, however, exclude certain properties and jobs from these calculations, despite the apparent lack of established industry policies with regard to this matter.

As previously stated, construction expenditures, which represent the base for capitalizing AFC under the prevailing funds expended method, are accumulated in work orders.[16] Many electric utilities, however, do not consider AFC for certain items and jobs for which work orders are issued. The questionnaire responses indicated that the following property and job items are excluded: (1) property ready for service;

---

[14] Long Island Lighting Company—Electric Rates, Case No. 26552, Opinion No. 75-1, Issued 9 January 1975.

[15] New York Public Service Commission, Technical Release Number 7 (Effective Immediately) Class A and B Utilities (Albany: the Commission, 28 January 1975).

[16] See pp. 68–69 of this chapter for a discussion of the topic. It is to be noted that the survey requested information on properties and jobs excluded from AFC considerations through an open-ended question rather than by asking about specific items. Consequently, any data reported might not be complete to the extent that the uilities responding to this question may not have indicated all the specific property and job items that they generally exclude from the expenditure base.

(2) property construction where service is not interrupted; (3) intangible plant; (4) land acquired for construction; (5) land held for future use; (6) blanket work orders; (7) work orders which do not exceed a certain minimum time period; and (8) work orders which do not exceed a certain minimum dollar amount. The exclusion of some of these items warrants further discussion.

PROPERTY READY FOR SERVICE. Of the 125 respondents which capitalize AFC, approximately 50 percent indicated that they omitted items of general plant from the calculation. These items are composed of assets unrelated to the production, transmission, or distribution functions of electric utilities. Examples are: (1) transportation equipment; (2) office furniture and equipment; (3) shop and garage equipment (tools); (4) laboratory equipment; and (5) communication equipment. In addition, many utilities exclude certain distribution items, such as meters and transformers; these are considered ready for service when acquired, which is ample justification for noncapitalization. To capitalize an allowance would not be consistent with the philosophy and purpose of the practice.

PROPERTY CONSTRUCTION WHERE SERVICE IS NOT MATERIALLY INTERRUPTED. Projects which occasion little or no interruption of service represent another type of property excluded from the AFC determination. These generally involve distribution facilities. Examples are: (1) general improvements to existing distribution facilities; (2) relocating or reconductoring existing lines; (3) rebuilding or rehabilitating existing lines; and (4) line conversions. Typically, service is not interrupted, and there is little or no loss of revenue to the utility involved. If service should be interrupted, it usually can be restored as the facilities are being reconstructed, rather than after they are completed. The foregoing reasons sufficiently justify the exclusion of these types of work orders from AFC determination.

INTANGIBLE PLANT. A number of utilities reported that they exclude capitalization of AFC on expenditures for plant costs on intangible assets. Specific examples listed included organization expenses, franchises, and leaseholds. Generally, these are not distributed to specific projects, jobs, or property units, nor are they depreciable. Furthermore, the cost of items such as leaseholds often are included in the utility's rate base when acquired.

LAND ACQUIRED FOR CONSTRUCTION. In many cases electric utilities purchase large amounts of land upon which to construct such facilities as generating plants, transmission lines, and substations. These acquisitions usually involve quite significant sums of money and can give rise to material amounts of capital costs. Land acquired for construction purposes raises a problem which is not present with other construction expenditures. Because land is a nondepreciable asset, its cost or any AFC capitalized on it cannot be recovered until it is disposed of through sale. This fact need not present any formidable barrier to capitalizing AFC on land acquired for construction, however. As pointed out by J. B. Madigan, a company can capitalize AFC on the total construction expenditure balance in a work order, including the land costs, and spread this allowance only over the depreciable assets accounts.[17] This procedure would give the utility the opportunity to recover its capital costs prior to the time the land is sold.

The practice of capitalizing AFC on land acquired for construction appears to be entirely consistent with the provisions in the uniform systems of accounts that stipulate AFC is a proper component of construction cost. Moreover, the commissions and courts have not ruled that land of this type should be excluded from the AFC calculation.

Of the 123 utilities responding to the question dealing with capitalizing AFC on land acquired for construction, 85 (69 percent) reported that they follow this practice.

LAND HELD FOR FUTURE USE. Although the capitalization of AFC on land used for construction appears perfectly acceptable, opinion is unclear regarding land held for future use. There are no provisions in the systems of accounts which in any way authorize capitalization of AFC on land of this type. Except for a 1931 Wisconsin case, which allowed capitalization on idle land for a certain period of time, no court or commission has permitted such capitalization prior to the period of construction.[18] Of the 121 electric companies responding to the question concerning this issue, only three stated that they followed the practice. Further investigation of these apparently positive responses, however, revealed that none capitalized AFC on this land while it was still considered property held for future use. Rather, the three firms began taking the allowance at the point when the land was devoted to a specific construction project. In effect, none of the questionnaire respondents

---

[17] Madigan, "Depreciation," p. 4.
[18] Re *Wisconsin Power and Light Company* (1931) P.U.R. 1931C 289.

capitalize AFC on land held for future use.[19]

MINIMUM DOLLAR AMOUNT OR TIME PERIOD WORK ORDERS. Electric utilities also exclude certain jobs subject to specific time and dollar limitations. These self-imposed restrictions have the effect of reducing the amount of AFC capitalized, and the amounts are sometimes quite substantial. For example, a large gas system conducted a review of its 1966 construction program and discovered that had the AFC capitalization rate been increased by three-quarters of one percent, the allowance for funds used during construction would have increased by about $100,000. If policies regarding time and dollar limitations had been revised, AFC would have increased by approximately $500,000 or more.[20] This seems to indicate that dollar limitation policies certainly are an important part of AFC considerations. One of the significant effects of these policies, which state that construction projects must exceed a minimum time and amount before AFC is capitalized, is that blanket work order projects often are excluded; these, by their nature, involve short time periods and relatively small amounts of money. Thus, utilities adhering to limitations policies generally confine capitalization of AFC to individual construction projects and specific construction work orders.

Analysis of the questionnaire responses reveals considerable variation among electric utilities' limitations policies.

A frequency tabulation of the utilities reporting *dollar* limitations is presented in Table 5. Of the 91 utilities responding, 24 percent excluded AFC on projects costing less than $5,000; 24 percent set $10,000 as the minimum; and 13 percent did not capitalize AFC on projects of less than $1,000. These three amounts represented about 61 percent of the total of those reporting. In addition to these 91 responses, 22 firms

---

19 In January 1971 the FPC amended its rules governing the accounting treatment of land held for future utility use. *Order No. 420* now permits land acquired under long-range planning to be included in the utility's rate base. In effect, this order eliminated the whole issue involving the capitalization of AFC on land held for future use. FPC, "Accounting Treatment for Land Held for Future Utility Use and for Profits or Losses Realized Through Sales of Those Lands," *Federal Register* 36 (14 January 1971): 507. The latest NARUC systems of accounts are virtually identical to those of the FPC. NARUC, *Uniform System of Accounts for Class A and B Electric Utilities,* 1972 (Washington, D.C.: the Association, 1972).

20 P. T. Harnack, "Mechanized and Expanded Interest During Construction," paper presented at the National Conference of Electric and Gas Utility Accountants, Miami Beach, Florida, 29–30 April and 1 May 1968, p. J-4.

replied that they had no minimum dollar limitation policy.

Some form of minimum *time* limitation policy was reported by 85 out of 120 companies responding to the questionnaire item. Results are summarized in Table 6. Of those 85 companies, approximately 72 percent used a thirty-day minimum, probably due to the fact that capitalized allowances usually are computed monthly. There was less variation among companies with regard to time as opposed to dollar limitation policies.

Of the 25 companies reporting no minimum time limitation policy, 9 set neither minimum time nor dollar limitations. This is shown in Table 7, which presents, in cross tabular form, data on responses to both time and dollar limitation policies. Table 7 seems to indicate that there is no significant relationship among these limitations.

TABLE 5.   Minimum Dollar Limitation Policies Reported in the Survey

Minimum dollar amount	Number of companies
$ 200	1
$ 750	1
$1,000	12
$1,500	2
$2,000	9
$2,500	2
$3,500	1
$5,000	22
$10,000	22
$20,000	3
$25,000	6
$50,000	5
$100,000	4
$200,000	1
Total	91

TABLE 6.   Minimum Time Limitation Policies Reported in the Survey

Minimum time period	Number of companies
30 days	61
60 days	15
90 days	8
6 months	1
Total	85

Table 7.   Cross Tabulation of Time and Dollar Limitations Responses Reported in the Survey

| Dollar limitations | Time limitations | | | | | | |
	None	30 days	60 days	90 days	6 months	Not ascertained	Total
None	9	11	1	0	1	0	22
$ 200	0	1	0	0	0	0	1
$ 750	1	0	0	0	0	0	1
$1,000	3	8	1	0	0	0	12
$1,500	1	1	0	0	0	0	2
$2,000	2	4	1	0	0	2	9
$2,500	1	0	0	0	0	1	2
$3,500	0	0	0	0	0	1	1
$5,000	3	14	3	2	0	0	22
$10,000	1	16	3	1	0	1	22
$20,000	0	2	1	0	0	0	3
$25,000	0	3	2	1	0	0	6
$50,000	1	0	2	2	0	0	5
$100,000	2	0	0	1	0	1	4
$200,000	1	0	0	0	0	0	1
Not ascertained	0	1	1	1	0	8	11
Total	25	61	15	8	1	14	124

Apparently, limitations policies are based upon practical grounds, namely, the administrative difficulties and accounting expense involved when AFC is computed on these exclusions. From a theoretical viewpoint, it should make no difference whether AFC is computed on construction projects involving long or short periods of time and large or small dollar outlays.[21] Rather, companies seem to utilize both types of limitations to ensure that construction projects which yield small allowances are not considered in determining the annual AFC amount capitalized.

The Time Period for Capitalizing AFC

Determining the proper time period during which allowance for funds used during construction is to be capitalized has presented many problems to both utility companies and commissions. Major disagreement has centered on attempts to determine the proper limits of the so-called

[21] Hatch, "Interest During Construction," p. 17.

construction period, that is, when it begins and ends. Instructions in the uniform systems of accounts for electric utilities state: " 'Allowance for funds used during construction' includes the net cost for the period of construction"; there is no further elaboration on or definition of the term.[22] Consequently, the task of determining the boundaries of this period has devolved, for the most part, upon the commissions and the courts.

Over the years, utility commissions have taken an active role in the problem of determining the proper capitalization period. In at least 19 jurisdictions, the respective commissions have specifically defined this period.[23] At the forefront has been the FPC, which has issued many opinions and orders regarding this question. Since cases heard by the FPC have dealt with many different aspects of determining the capitalization period, reviewing these opinions and orders should contribute to an understanding of some of the major problems involved.

BEGINNING OF CONSTRUCTION PERIOD. The matter of identifying the beginning of the construction period for capitalization purposes probably has received more attention than any other aspect of the more general AFC problem. This is due to the fact that there are many measures which must be taken by a utility prior to the incurrence of actual construction expenditures. For example, years before actual construction begins, large sums of money may be expended on land acquisitions and preliminary engineering and general business surveys. Project No. 637 of the Chelan Electric Company is a case in point. Although active construction began on about 1 January 1926, the licensee claimed that there was continuous preliminary investigation and land acquisition from 3 September 1907.[24] The FPC disallowed this contention and set the beginning date of the period three years prior to the initiation of active construction as a reasonable time span in which to carry out the necessary preliminary work. This three-year maximum, established by the commission in a number of other cases as well,[25] was not arbitrary.

---

[22] FPC, *Uniform System*, p. 101-7.

[23] FPC, *Federal and State Commission Jurisdiction and Regulation of Electric and Gas Utilities*, 1973 (Washington, D.C.: U.S. Government Printing Office, 1973), p. 65.

[24] *Chelan Electric Co.* (1933) 1 FPC 91, 95.

[25] *Re Northern States Power Co.* (1939) 1 FPC 597; *Re Inland Power and Light Co.* (1942) 3 FPC 321; and *Portland General Electric Company* (1934) 1 FPC 169.

A maximum of three years also was set for a preliminary permit issued to the licensee of a hydroelectric project under the Federal Water Power Act of 1920 and the Federal Power Act of 1935.[26] The commission, however, has not allowed a three-year preliminary construction period in all cases. An opinion involving the Kanawha Valley Power Company stated: "The construction period is defined as including a period reasonably necessary for the performance of preliminary work absolutely essential to eliminate wasteful expenditures and delays in the subsequent development."[27] The commission concluded that the construction period should be determined by the evidence of records in each particular case; as a result, in this opinion it allowed a one-year maximum for the preliminary work.[28] While it is evident that the FPC generally sees fit to include as part of the construction period preliminary activities up to a maximum of three years prior to active construction, it is also clear that each case is judged individually. Determination seems to be based not on how long the period is, but on how long it should be, assuming that the preliminary activities are performed on a reasonably continuous basis. Since it is recognized that these activities are as essential in bringing the required service to the customers as the active construction itself, this preliminary period properly should be included in the construction period for the purposes of capitalizing AFC.

The effect of these decisions on electric utilities can be assessed by analyzing the responses to question seven in the survey: 50 respondents reported capitalizing AFC on preliminary survey and investigation charges, while 75 reported they did not. The large number of negative responses may be somewhat misleading; many companies may not incur these expenditures in material amounts and, for this reason alone, do not bother to capitalize AFC on these charges. Of those that do capitalize allowances on these charges, it is difficult to discern any clear pattern of when computation begins. Approximately 25 percent indicated they capitalize allowances either when the preliminary survey begins or on a retroactive basis when active construction commences. However, the majority of those not capitalizing stated that they began doing so sometime after the charges were transferred to the construction job order,

26 Phillips, *Economics*, pp. 565–66.
27 *Kanawha Valley Power Co.* (1936) 1 FPC 327.
28 Ibid.

that is, sometime subsequent to the start of active construction. Only three companies mentioned a specific time period prior to active construction when they began capitalization: In two cases this was three years prior to construction, and in one case, one year. It appears that the early FPC decisions have had little influence on the current policies of utilities in the sense that firms wait until active construction commences on the project before any AFC is capitalized.

END OF CONSTRUCTION PERIOD. The end of the construction period, and concomitant cessation of AFC capitalization, also has been given much consideration by the commissions and the courts. Since the earliest cases it clearly has been established that capitalization should cease on the date or dates when the project becomes available for its intended use.[29] This standard has the effect of precluding capitalization of AFC when a project is rendering service, but clean-up construction work still is in progress. As succinctly stated by the FPC: "Not merely its technical physical functioning, but the nature of the use for which it is designed and its adequacy to meet the burdens such use entails are factors to be considered in determining the date the project can be regarded as available for operation."[30] Thus, the availability of the property for operations, regardless of the fact that certain construction activities continue or that the property is not yet earning an adequate return, is the key factor in some of the earlier decisions. With the passage of time, the commission appears to have taken a somewhat less rigid position, similar to its stand regarding the start of the construction period. For example: "Determination of the date upon which the capitalization of interest and taxes during construction should cease is not controlled by artificial rules, is not a matter of formula but is a matter of reasonable judgment based on a consideration of all the pertinent facts; and neither full capacity generation nor the completion of all construction activities, nor the making of permanent installations, as against those of a temporary nature, are absolutely necessary with respect to this determination."[31] Through this decision, the FPC recognized the need for a more flexible approach in handling timing problems.

---

[29] *Chelan Electric Co.* (1933) 1 FPC 102, 105; and *Re Clarion River Power Co.* (1935) 1 FPC 270, 286.
[30] *Louisville Hydro-Electric Co.* (1933) 1 FPC 150.
[31] *Re Pennsylvania Water and Power Co.* (1949) 82 PUR NS 193.

A closely related question involves when AFC should cease to be capitalized if the project is a multiple-unit one with different completion dates, and a portion is determined to be in service prior to completion of the entire project. The FPC addressed this issue in the *Safe Harbor Water Power Corporation* case.[32] The licensee had installed six units under one project: The first went into service in December 1931, three more were operating by the end of January 1932, the fifth was in operation twenty months later, and four months after that the final unit was in service. Safe Harbor wanted to lump together the allowance for the construction period for all the units, without consideration of the individual completion dates. The firm proposed the average date of 1 July 1932 as the beginning of commercial operation and the point at which capitalized AFC should cease. The commission rejected this date as hypothetical; stating that commercial operation began when the first four units were in condition to deliver dependable power, it set 29 February 1932 as the cut-off point for capitalization. In effect, the decision maintained that, on a multiple-unit project, AFC should cease on the basis of actual unit completion and availability for service, and not on some arbitrary measure.

This reasoning eventually was incorporated as a note in the uniform systems of accounts for electric utilities prescribed by both the FPC and NARUC. In explaining allowance for funds used during construction in Utility Plant Instruction 3 (17), the systems of accounts contain the following:

> Note—When a part only of a plant or project is placed in operation or is completed and ready for service but the construction work as a whole is incomplete, that part of the cost of the property placed in operation, or ready for service shall be treated as "Utility Plant in Service" and allowance for funds used during construction thereon as a charge to construction shall cease. Allowance for funds used during construction on that part of the cost of the plant which is incomplete may be continued as a charge to construction until such time as it is placed in operation or is ready for service, except as limited in item 17, above.[33]

An examination of the responses to questionnaire item thirteen, deal-

[32] *Safe Harbor Water Power Corp.* (1935) 1 FPC 249.
[33] FPC, *Uniform System*, p. 101-7, as revised; and NARUC, *Uniform System*, p. 15.

ing with multiple-unit projects, reveals the following: Of the 97 utilities reporting projects with partial service available prior to completion, 91 stated that they, in effect, discontinued capitalization on the portion placed in service but continued taking it on that portion not in service. Only three ceased capitalizing AFC on the entire project when the first portion went into service. It is quite evident that the electric utilities adhere closely to the rule set forth in the uniform systems of accounts.

FPC ACCOUNTING RELEASE NUMBER AR-5. In December 1964 the FPC issued the first of several accounting releases, the purpose of which was to express and disseminate informal interpretations of the uniform systems of accounts by the commission's chief accountant.[34] These releases offer accounting guidelines for certain items for which previous instructions were either vague or nonexistent. The fifth of these, *Accounting Release Number AR-5*, presents the views of the chief accountant as to the proper period for capitalizing AFC.[35]

Federal Power Commission
Accounting Release Number AR-5

Question:
What is the proper period for capitalization of interest during construction?

Answer:
Interest during construction may be capitalized starting from the date that construction costs are continuously incurred on a planned progressive basis. Interest should not be accrued for the period prior to: (1) the date of issuance of the preliminary permit by the Commission of a licensed hydroelectric project; and (2) the date of the application to the Commission for a certificate to construct facilities by a natural gas company. Interest accruals may be allowed by the Commission for the period prior to the above dates if so justified by the company. No interest should be accrued during periods of interrupted construction unless the company can justify the interruption as being reasonable under the circumstances.

Capitalization of interest stops when the facilities have been tested

---

[34] FPC, "FPC's Chief Accountant Issues First in New Series of Accounting Releases Reestablishing Policy Dropped in 1942," News Release No. 13598, 30 December 1964, 2 pages.
[35] FPC, *Accounting Release Number AR-5* (Washington, D.C.: the Commission, 10 November 1965).

and are placed in service. This would include those portions of construction projects completed and put into service although the project is not fully completed. Should the test period exceed thirty days, the company must submit full particulars and justification for an extension of such period to the Commission in Accordance with Plant Instruction 9.D.

Arthur L. Litke

Effective:
November 10, 1965

On 20 February 1968 the FPC announced a revision of AR-5, effective 1 January 1968. The change involved altering the wording in the first sentence of the second paragraph from "capitalization of interest stops when the facilities have been tested and are *placed in service*" to "capitalization of interest stops when the facilities have been tested and are *placed in or ready for service.*" The purpose was to bring the wording of AR-5 in line with that of Electric Plant Instruction 3 (17) of the uniform system which uses the phrase "ready for service." Apparently, a number of interested parties viewed "placed in service" as a substitute for "ready for service," when the original intent in AR-5 was to consider them synonymous. The effect of the revision was to change the termination date for capitalizing AFC to the date it either was ready for service or placed in service, whichever was earlier.

Accounting Release Number AR-5 is essentially a reconfirmation of the FPC's existing policies. Presenting no new guidelines, the *Release* merely synopsizes previous commission opinions and orders dealing with the capitalization period. For example, the statement in the *Release* that no interest should be accrued during periods of interrupted construction, unless the interruption can be justified as reasonable, is the logical result of prior commission decisions on this matter.[36] The *Release* is sufficiently general to avoid specifically limiting the capitalization period to any artificial or arbitrary boundaries and to permit determination of the period to be based upon the facts in a particular case.

---

[36] *Florida Power Corporation* (1937) 1 FPC 390, 403; and *Puget Sound Power and Light Co.* v. *Federal Power Commission* (1943) 50 PUR (NS) 375, 78 U.S. App. D.C. 143, 137 F (2d) 701.

Determination of Capitalization Rates

Historically, a great deal of unresolved controversy has existed between the electric utilities and the FPC regarding the proper rate to be applied in capitalizing AFC. Consequently, there is still no generally accepted basis for determining that rate. The dispute extends to the very purpose and philosophy of capitalizing AFC.

A major source of controversy is the ambiguous wording in the instructions of the uniform systems of accounts regarding AFC. Paragraph 3 (17) of the Utility Plant Instructions states, in part: "Allowance for funds used during construction includes the net cost for the period of construction of borrowed funds used for construction purposes and a reasonable rate on other funds when so used."[37] This statement implies that it is possible to identify precisely the amounts of borrowed and other funds applied to specific construction projects; the inference is that the AFC capitalization rates can be based on the cost of these specific funds. Most utilities, however, would find it extremely difficult to differentiate these sources since they rarely earmark and segregate specific funds for construction purposes. More usually, a going concern financing expansion will utilize a general pool of cash, the sources of which constantly change. The pool ordinarily contains funds from (1) borrowing, (2) new equity capital, (3) operations or retained earnings, (4) depreciation charges, and (5) other various noncash credits, such as deferred taxes.[38] Thus, when these funds are comingled and used for construction of specific projects, it is almost impossible to compute the exact amount of AFC associated with each source.[39] Further complicating the matter is the fact that some of the funds themselves, such as those generated from depreciation and retained earnings, are very difficult to trace because they also are composites of different types of funds.[40] As a result, both the utilities and the FPC have been forced to use estimates and approximations. The major point in the disagreement

---

[37] FPC, *Uniform System*, p. 101-7, as revised.

[38] Homer E. Sayad, "An Accountant Looks at Capitalized Interest," paper presented at the National Conference of Electric and Gas Utility Accountants, New Orleans, Louisiana, 2–4 May 1966, p. G5.

[39] Ferd Rydell, "Interest During Construction," Part II, *Public Utilities Fortnightly* 89 (25 May 1967): 28.

[40] Arthur Andersen and Co., *Principles Underlying the Capitalization of Interest During Construction* (Chicago: the Company, 1953), pp. 14–15.

between the two has been over what factors, consistent with the uniform systems of accounts, should be considered in determining proper estimates for the capitalization rates.

THE FPC POSITION. Prior to August 1971 the FPC maintained that it was the intent of the systems of accounts, in using the word *interest* in the term "interest during construction," to endorse a pure interest concept; thus, the commission believed that any rate used in capitalizing AFC should not exceed a normal interest rate. This philosophy is reflected in numerous opinions and orders which ruled that utilities could use as rates for capitalizing AFC the actual cost of debt capital used in construction and a maximum 6 percent rate on other funds.[41]

The one opinion which best set forth the views of the FPC in this matter was the *Northern Natural Gas Company* case,[42] which involved a rate proceeding. The FPC allowed Northern Natural an 8.75 percent return on its common equity in determining the fair rate of return on rate base, but for purposes of capitalizing AFC it limited the allowed capitalization rate of the company's own funds to a maximum of 6 percent. For many years prior to this decision, Northern Natural had capitalized AFC on its books using an overall rate of 6 percent based upon work order balances extending longer than 30 days, which procedure had been approved by the FPC in an earlier original cost investigation.[43] In the course of the rate case hearings, however, the commission's staff made a number of presentations and contentions which supported a reduction in this rate. The FPC's decision was based mainly on its staff's presentations and clearly reflected the commission's attitude, a portion of which is presented below.

> *Interest during Construction*: Paragraph 5 (17), Gas Plant Accounts—Instructions of our Uniform System of Accounts Prescribed for Natural Gas Companies sets forth our policy with respect to

---

[41] *Re Puget Sound Power and Light Co.* (1942) 45 PUR (NS) 237; *Re Transcontinental Gas Pipe Line Corp.* (1952) 94 PUR NS 333; *Kansas State Corp. Commission v. Federal Power Commission* (1953) 1 PUR 3d 310, 206 F2d 690; and *South Carolina Generating Co. v. Federal Power Commission* (1958) 27 PUR 3d 198, 261, F2d 915.

[42] *Re Northern Natural Gas Co.* (1952) 95 PUR NS 289.

[43] Ernest B. Blease, "Interest During Construction and Its Relation to Rate of Return," paper presented at the National Conference of Electric and Gas Utility Accountants, Chicago, Illinois, 20–22 April 1953, p. 727.

interest during construction as follows: "Interest during construction includes a net cost of borrowed funds used for construction purposes and a reasonable rate upon the Utility's own funds when so used." [As expressed in the FPC's uniform system of accounts for natural gas companies in effect prior to August 1971.] In accordance therewith, we have generally allowed the actual cost of borrowed funds and a 6% rate of interest on corporate funds used for construction purposes. It had been our practice to refuse to allow the capitalization of interest during construction at rates which would result in a high profit during construction for the allowance is not for the purpose of providing the company with a fair rate of return before operations begin. It should be noted that the quoted Instruction relates to "interest." We believe that 6% is the maximum rate that can be claimed in these times.

During the year 1950, the major part of the construction funds was provided by the issuance of $40,000,000 of 2⅝% serial debentures at an effective interest rate of 2.66% and by 2% short-term bank loans at $13,000,000. $9,591,750 was also raised by the issuance of 304,000 shares of $10 par value common stock. These equity funds, the record shows, were used only during the first three and last three months of 1950, and from March, 1950, to October, 1950, the borrowed funds were used.

Notwithstanding the facts respecting the use of the funds for construction purposes, Northern has applied an over-all rate of 6% which, when broken down by classes of funds, provides a rate of 10% on the equity funds. Obviously 10% is an unreasonable rate for interest.[44]

In essence, the FPC interpreted the systems of accounts very narrowly so as to allow only a maximum 6 percent rate on equity funds. Apparently, the commission believed that, had the systems of accounts intended the capitalization rate to reflect more than an interest concept, this would have been provided by allowing as part of the utility plant cost a fair return concept on property under construction. Since this was not done, the commission believed that it would have been improper to stretch the meaning of the word *interest* to imply more than that attributed to its ordinary connotation.

THE OPPOSITION. The FPC's position in the *Northern Natural* case was strongly criticized by many utility representatives, who considered the opinion unfair and unrealistic. Their opposition was not confined to

----

[44] *Re Northern Natural Gas Co.* (1952) 95 PUR NS 299.

the decision itself, but extended to the underlying rationale upon which it was based.

Those representing the utilities believed that it was not the intent of the systems of accounts to restrict the capitalization rate to a narrow *interest* interpretation. They argued that by allowing the 6 percent rate on equity funds at a time when debt funds carried lower interest rates, the FPC in effect also was recognizing a broader concept of *interest*, one which included a return element. Yet, it was not understood how the commission allowed Northern a return of 8.75 percent on equity funds after the plant was in service, as opposed to 6 percent during the construction period. This apparent inconsistency must have stemmed from the commission's belief that capitalizing the costs on equity funds used for construction and including them in the rate base reduced the risk involved in recovering these costs.[45] Opponents considered the commission's reasoning fallacious because these equity costs could be recovered only through future depreciation, regardless of when they were capitalized; thus, they were subject to at least the same risks as all equity capital.[46] Hence, the utilities believed the commission had erred in applying a lower return rate for equity capital used during construction, when a higher return rate was allowed on the same capital after the plant went into service.

Those representing the utility interests were not the only ones who disagreed with the FPC opinion. During the 1940s and 1950s, many state commissions were allowing utilities to use an overall rate of 5–6 percent in capitalizing AFC. Since the cost of borrowed funds was considerably less than this amount, there was tacit approval on the part of these commissions that other funds should have been capitalized at something greater than the maximum 6 percent rate allowed by the FPC. In 1967, the Nevada Public Service Commission, in issuing a rate order in the Southwest Gas Corporation application, openly criticized the FPC's stand. "In establishing a reasonable rate on other funds, the record reveals that the FPC, with only a few minor exceptions, has consistently used a figure of six per cent. We view this approach as highly arbitrary, particularly in light of the ever-fluctuating market from which common equity funds must be obtained. Such being the case, we are not disposed to follow the FPC pattern of automatically equating six per

---

[45] Madigan, "Depreciation," p. 4.
[46] Sayad, "Capitalized Interest," p. 6.

cent with 'a reasonable rate on other funds when so used.' "[47] To the extent that this allowance was too low adequately to compensate the utility for all its capital costs incurred during construction, the utility would be prevented from recovering all of its costs through future revenues.

BASES FOR CAPITALIZATION RATES. The capitalization rates used by utilities during the past 25 years and the foundations upon which these rates supposedly were established in many instances do not seem supported by substantive bases. Admittedly, some of the blame can be attributed to the ambiguous instructions regarding interest during construction then found in the systems of accounts and to the somewhat unreasonable attitude of the FPC, as exemplified in the *Northern Natural Gas* case. Yet, much of the fault also can be ascribed to the utility industry itself for not attempting long ago to establish definitive and sound methods upon which to determine capitalization rates.

Past surveys clearly point out the impact the FPC/utility controversy has had on attempts to develop sound capitalization rates. For example, a survey conducted in 1948 by H. B. Hardwick of New Orleans Public Service, Inc., revealed that, of 52 utilities that capitalized AFC, only 27 were using a cost of capital or rate of return concept as an underlying basis. Of the remainder, 16 companies claimed that they based their rate upon the cost of borrowed funds only, while 9 stated that the basis for the rate used was "arbitrary."[48] A 1962 survey reported that 27 out of 45 respondents were using a cost of capital or rate of return basis for the capitalization rate. The remaining companies used various other bases, among them: (1) management discretion; (2) the approximate cost of borrowed money; (3) 5 percent; (4) a rate equal to the rate on the last bond issue; (5) prime rate cost of short-term money; (6) a conservative rate less than the cost of capital and the allowable rate of return; (7) "rates used were determined during 1953 based on written experience gained in dealings with the Federal Power Commission. No written instructions. The State Commission had indicated that 5% was too low but has not issued any written instructions."[49] At least 4 other

---

[47] *Re Southwest Gas Corporation* (1967) 69 PUR 3d 364.

[48] H. B. Hardwick, "Survey on Interest During Construction" (New Orleans: New Orleans Public Service, Inc., 8 April 1948), 4 pages.

[49] General Accounting Committee, American Gas Association and Edison Electric Institute, *Questionnaire—Interest During Construction*, 20 November 1962, pp. 3–6.

utilities reported that they capitalized AFC using a maximum rate of 6 percent on equity funds used for construction.[50]

The authors' survey, conducted in 1970, established that many utilities justified their rates on bases inconsistent with the underlying theory, philosophy, or purpose of capitalizing AFC. For example, of the 120 responses to the question regarding the basis for the rate, 37 companies listed some type of cost of borrowed money concept. Another 4 said their basis was what the state regulatory commission allows, and one listed the "trend of the industry." The remaining 78 reported that they used some sort of cost of capital or rate of return basis.

Obviously, during the past 25 years the electric utilities and some regulatory commissions, particularly the FPC until very recently, have not applied thorough analysis or sound reasoning in their attempts to develop a proper AFC capitalization rate.[51] Continued use of such irrational rate bases could mean that high current costs of capital incurred in financing construction would fail to be properly considered in the AFC computation. In 1967 the electric utilities faced just such an industry-wide situation. The fact that 1967 was apparently the first time for such an occurrence partially may explain why many utilities seemed so unconcerned about the matter in the past.

THE CAPITALIZATION RATES USED. The authors' survey contained a question regarding actual rates used by electric utilities in capitalizing AFC during the five-year period 1966–1970. Replies revealed that, beginning in 1968, there was a substantial movement toward the use of higher rates. Concerning actual 1966 rates, 96 of 116 electric utilities reported using the traditional 6 percent; only 2 used a rate in excess of that. In 1967, the upward movement began. Of 115 utilities, 104 listed

---

[50] Ibid.

[51] Note that in 1966 the FPC did change its stand on allowing a maximum rate of 6 percent on other funds by deciding to accept, without the necessity for extensive justification on the part of the utilities, an overall capitalization rate of 6 percent. In analyzing the reason for the shift, it does not appear, however, that the change reflected a new thinking on the commission's part as much as an intention to bring about a simplification of its reviews and audits. The 6 percent figure was derived from the fact that it represented the maximum rate that other commissions were allowing at that time. The most recent development by the FPC is in their proposed rulemaking Docket No. RM75-27, dated 20 May 1975, in which a specific formula for calculating AFC is suggested. *Federal Register* 40 (29 May 1975): 23322–33. This formula is discussed and elaborated upon in note 57 below.

6 percent, and 5 others a rate in excess of that amount. By 1968 the traditional 6 percent was virtually abandoned. Of 120 utilities reporting, 76 listed rates in excess of 6 percent, including 48 firms using 6.5 percent, and 15 using 7 percent or more. The main cause underlying this sharp increase was the substantial rise in 1968 of the capital costs of financing construction. The cost, which was almost 7 percent, had risen approximately one percent above the 1967 figure. The reason most utilities continued to use 6.5 percent despite even higher money costs in mid-1968 was the FPC's refusal to accept a higher rate without substantive proof of need from the utility.[52]

During 1969 and 1970 these financing costs continued to rise, and electric utilities were forced to increase their capitalization rates on construction funds. Questionnaire responses show that in 1969 only 49 of 120 companies were using a rate of 6.5 percent or less, with 34 of these using exactly 6.5 percent. An additional 54 utilities reported rates between 6.5 and 7 percent, 40 of these at 7 percent. The remaining 17 listed rates in excess of 7 percent, 8 of these being 7.5 percent. Responses for 1970 revealed a continued rise. Only 21 of 121 reporting utilities gave a figure of less than 7 percent. Of the remainder, there were 40 companies with rates between 7 and 7.5 percent; 35 at exactly 7.5 percent; and 25 in excess of 7.5 percent (13 using 8 percent and 6 using 8.5 percent).

In analyzing the upward revision it is quite obvious that these rates did not cover the rapidly rising capital costs. For example, in 1968, when the cost of senior capital to the electric utilities hovered at 7 percent and the cost of equity capital was considerably higher, most firms were capitalizing AFC at less than 7 percent. Likewise, for 1969 and 1970, when debt costs alone soared to ranges of from 8.5 to over 10 percent, the corresponding capitalization rates continued to lag considerably.

Determining an Acceptable AFC Rate

In viewing some of the above problems it clearly is imperative that an acceptable capitalization rate for calculating allowance for funds used during construction be determined. The previous discussion shows the lack of progress in achieving this goal. A major factor has been the

---

[52] Duff and Phelps, Inc., *Survey* (18 July 1969), p. 1.

failure to develop a rational framework on an industry-wide basis. Had such criteria previously been available, much confusion and misunderstanding could have been avoided.[53] With continued increases in construction and capital costs during the 1960s and 1970s, interested parties have been forced to recognize that the haphazard approaches used in the past are no longer adequate or acceptable.

Any attempt to develop sound and reasonable AFC rates must be founded upon suitable standards or principles. The general guidelines which follow seek to establish this foundation. The principles are consistent with sound economic objectives and the instructions regarding AFC as presently stated in the uniform systems of accounts. The general nature of these statements will provide any utility adequate direction in establishing an acceptable and reasonable AFC capitalization rate.

First, any rate developed should be consistent with the purpose for capitalizing AFC. It should be devised to compensate a utility for its overall capital costs incurred to finance construction and should be based solely on this premise.

Second, since positive identification of specific fund sources devoted to construction projects is in most cases unfeasible and unrealistic, appropriate estimates of *all* component capital costs of construction must be included in developing proper rate components.

Third, each utility that capitalizes AFC should develop its own overall capitalization rate as well as rate components based upon its own experienced costs of capital. Fixed or set rates *never* should be adopted or assigned to any group of utilities.

Fourth, since rate components are necessarily estimates, they should not vary too much or to often. The overall rate, therefore, should be based upon an average of costs over a period of time so as to smooth out sharp fluctuations.

Fifth, a rate component should not be unwieldy in its calculation, but should lend itself to easy verification and audit for purposes of determining the legality, propriety, and reasonableness of the overall rate.

Earlier discussion clearly indicated that in establishing AFC capitalization rates many utilities resort to unsystematic approaches apparently based upon management discretion and expediency rather than upon some logical framework. The use of guidelines such as those presented above will afford utilities a better opportunity to establish and use AFC

---

[53] For example, *Re Northern Natural Gas Company* (1952) 95 PUR NS 299.

rates which more closely approximate their real capital costs of construction. A methodology now will be suggested for developing an overall AFC rate; if properly applied, the method can produce a reasonable rate which satisfies the necessary requirement of approximating the true capital costs of construction and also one consistent with the suggested guidelines. What is involved is the identification of specific fund sources available, regardless of their ultimate use, weighted to the total funds available. These weightings then are applied to reasonable component rates or costs for each fund source, summed to arrive at a sound and reasonable weighted AFC rate.

SOURCES OF FUNDS. Funds are available from a number of sources. External funds generally are provided by the issuance of new securities: short- and long-term debt and preferred and common stock. Internally generated funds arise from retained earnings (net income less cash dividends), depreciation and amortization, deferred income taxes, and deferred investment tax credits. A utility's Statement of Source and Application of Funds or the now widely used Statement of Sources of Funds Used for Construction Expenditures provides a useful identification tool. A hypothetical Statement of Sources of Funds Used for Construction Expenditures is found in Table 8.[54] An analysis of the sources shown will determine the amounts available throughout the period being analyzed and provide the basis to which rate components are applied. The table gives information for a four-year period.

ANALYSIS OF SOURCES OF FUNDS. The first item in Table 8 shows the year-end accumulation of reinvested retained earnings for each accounting period. In 1970 these amounted to $9,200; 1971, $4,500; 1972, $10,300; and in 1973, $16,300. However, the total dollars of reinvested earnings as shown on the period end statement were not available throughout the year. Since the funds statement does not explain the period of time during which the reinvested earnings were available, a separate calculation must be made. This is determined by reviewing the history of the retained earnings credits during each year. Table 9 provides this analysis on a monthly basis. The monthly changes may represent additions to or withdrawals from the account, or the net effect of both. The additions represent the net income for the subperiods, while the withdrawals, shown in parentheses, are either losses, dividend pay-

---

[54] The same information easily can be derived from the more traditional Statement of Changes in Financial Position (Statement of Sources and Application of Funds).

ments, or other charges to retained earnings. When calculating the average amount outstanding throughout the year, the general practice is to use a thirteen-month weighted average, by month; this provides a reasonable approximation and gives proper recognition for funds available for a greater period of time throughout the year.

The actual calculations are as follows: (1) The January change (addition or net withdrawal) is recorded. This amount also represents the

TABLE 8.   Statement of Sources of Funds Used for Construction Expenditures

Source	1970	1971	1972	1973
Funds generated internally				
Reinvested earnings:				
Net income	$34,000	$30,100	$36,800	$47,500
Less cash dividends	25,200	25,600	26,500	31,200
	$ 9,200	$ 4,500	$10,300	$16,300
Principal noncash items:				
Depreciation	$21,000	$23,500	$26,000	$28,400
Deferred income tax, net	1,900	3,300	5,700	5,600
Deferred investment tax credit, net	2,000	600	3,100	1,300
Allowance for funds used				
during construction	(5,000)	(3,900)	(4,100)	(6,200)
Total	$19,900	$23,500	$30,700	$29,100
Funds from outside sources				
Long-term debt	$40,000	$50,000	$50,000	$ —
Common stock	—	—	29,000	36,600
Preferred stock	—	—	—	30,000
Notes payable (less repayments)	(1,500)	(7,100)	(31,400)	14,000
Net change in working capital				
and other items[a]	5,700	4,100	(1,100)	2,500
Total	$44,200	$47,000	$46,500	$83,100
Total internal and external funds	$73,300	$75,000	$87,500	$128,500
Allowance for funds used				
during construction	5,000	3,900	4,100	6,200
Total funds used for construc-				
tion expenditures	$78,300	$78,900	$91,600	$134,700

NOTE: As calculated from Annual Financial Statements.
[a] This item, often shown in Funds Statements, is a balancing figure and is not to be interpreted as a source of construction funds.

TABLE 9.   Reinvested Earnings (Net Income Less Dividends), in Dollars

Period	1970	1971	1972	1973
January	(1590)	(1740)	(6300)	(2120)
Year to date	(1590)	(1740)	(6300)	(2120)
February	5600	5840	5730	4680
Year to date	4010	4100	(570)	2560
March	5200	4310	5600	3880
Year to date	9210	8410	5030	6440
April	(2470)	(4000)	(3480)	(2220)
Year to date	6740	4410	1550	4220
May	3100	1060	2710	1000
Year to date	9840	5470	4260	5220
June	2750	370	1650	2270
Year to date	12590	5840	5910	7490
July	(4270)	(3700)	(2810)	(4100)
Year to date	8320	2140	3100	3390
August	1060	(910)	1470	3830
Year to date	9380	1230	4570	7220
September	950	1680	3780	5710
Year to date	10330	2910	8350	12930
October	(5730)	(1430)	(900)	(3900)
Year to date	4600	1480	7450	9030
November	2730	2910	200	3710
Year to date	7330	4390	7650	12740
December	1870	110	2650	3560
Year to date	9200	4500	10300	16300
Monthly totals year to dates	89960	43140	51300	85420
1/13 weighted average	6920	3318	3946	6571

year-to-date for January. (2) The next month's change (February) is added, and a year-to-date total is calculated. (3) The procedure outlined in step 2 is repeated through the month of December, calculating year-to-date balances after each month's change. (4) The December year-to-date amount is the figure displayed in the funds statement. (5) Year-to-date totals, January through December, are summed. (6) One-thirteenth of the total year-to-date summation is calculated. (This calculation assumes a *zero* balance as of 1 January 19_____ and each subsequent year.) The one-thirteenth of the total provides a weighted figure of reinvested earnings available for construction throughout the fiscal year.

A similar set of calculations is illustrated in Table 10 for arriving at a weighted average for depreciation. Although the detail is not shown, the same procedures are followed for calculating average deferred income tax and deferred investment tax credit figures.

Weighted averages also must be calculated for any outside financing gained through the sales of long-term debt and/or common and/or preferred stock. Table 11 provides an illustration as it applies to long-term debt. The calculation is performed using the same steps as outlined above for retained earnings. Use the same approach for calculating common and preferred stock issues throughout the year.

Calculating annual average available funds provided by notes payable (short-term debt due within one year) presents a slightly different problem. This source is essentially a revolving fund which may turn over several times in a given accounting period. Thus, the December balance shown on the funds statement does not represent a year-to-date total or an accumulation throughout the period, but merely an outstanding amount at the period end, 31 December. A simple thirteen-month average of the monthly balances—December of the previous year through December of the current year—produces an acceptable average of the outstanding funds. Table 12 illustrates the procedure.

Once weighted average balances are calculated for all fund sources, percentages of weighted average dollars by source to total weighted average dollars from all sources of construction investment are derived. Table 13, column C, shows these results.

DETERMINING RATE COMPONENTS. While the ultimate objective is to develop an annual overall AFC rate based on funds effectively available over the entire period, it is first necessary to develop individual fund source rate components. Furthermore, it must be recognized that it is impossible to calculate a precise overall rate.

TABLE 10. Depreciation, in Dollars

Period	1970	1971	1972	1973
January	1750	1950	2100	2500
Year to date	1750	1950	2100	2500
February	1700	1960	2090	2540
Year to date	3450	3910	4190	5040
March	1670	1980	2040	2550
Year to date	5120	5890	6230	7590
April	1620	2000	1980	2550
Year to date	6740	7890	8210	10140
May	1690	1860	2020	2540
Year to date	8430	9750	10230	12680
June	1710	1860	2080	2540
Year to date	10140	11610	12310	15220
July	1710	1900	2090	2470
Year to date	11850	13510	14400	17690
August	1760	1920	2190	1240
Year to date	13610	15430	16590	18930
September	1790	1930	2300	2460
Year to date	15400	17360	18890	21390
October	1820	2150	2370	2300
Year to date	17220	19510	21260	23690
November	1870	1930	2400	2350
Year to date	19090	21440	23660	26040
December	1910	2060	2340	2360
Year to date	21000	23500	26000	28400
Monthly totals year to dates	133800	151750	164070	189310
1/13 weighted average	10292	11673	12621	14562

NOTE: Similar calculations are performed for deferred income taxes and deferred investment tax credits.

TABLE 11. Sale of Long-term Debt, in Dollars

Period	1970	1971	1972	1973
January	—	15000	—	—
Year to date	—	15000	—	—
February	10000	—	—	—
Year to date	10000	15000	—	—
March	—	—	—	—
Year to date	10000	15000	—	—
April	10000	15000	—	—
Year to date	20000	30000	—	—
May	—	5000	—	—
Year to date	20000	35000	—	—
June	—	—	—	—
Year to date	20000	35000	—	—
July	10000	—	25000	—
Year to date	30000	35000	25000	—
August	—	10000	—	—
Year to date	30000	45000	25000	—
September	—	5000	—	—
Year to date	30000	50000	25000	—
October	5000	—	—	—
Year to date	35000	50000	25000	—
November	5000	—	—	—
Year to date	40000	50000	25000	—
December	—	—	25000	—
Year to date	40000	50000	50000	—
Monthly totals year to dates	285000	425000	175000	—
1/13 Weighted average	21923	32692	13462	—

NOTE: Similar calculations are performed for issues of new common and preferred stock.

The appropriate rate to be applied to each fund source must be based upon the current costs of these funds. The current cost of debt capital is the weighted annual rate for debt capital issued during the year. The same criterion is appropriate for preferred stock with a fixed dividend rate.

Determination of a proper rate for common equity, including new stock issues as well as reinvested retained earnings, is more difficult. A reasonable suggestion is the currently authorized return on common equity as prescribed by a utility's regulatory commission. During periods of frequent rate-case negotiation, this latter will present no problems; however, during periods of infrequent hearings, assurance must be obtained that the rate is not outdated—is not too high or too low.

Rates to be applied to internally generated funds also must be determined. Funds arising from depreciation and amortization represent a composite of previous investment from all funds used, and the cost rate applied to these should be based upon an overall rate of return. That rate is based on the one established in the most recent rate proceeding, which again should be checked for currency. The funds represented by

TABLE 12. Notes Payable (Due within One Year)

Period	1970			1971		
	Balance	Rate	Interest	Balance	Rate	Interest
December						
(prior year)	$ 40,000	7.95%	$ 3,180.00	$ 38,500	9.00%	$ 3,465.00
January	39,500	8.30	3,278.50	38,500	9.00	3,465.00
February	43,000	8.50	3,655.00	38,500	9.00	3,465.00
March	43,000	8.50	3,655.00	45,000	8.75	3,937.50
April	41,200	8.75	3,605.00	39,500	8.75	3,456.25
May	39,700	9.00	3,573.00	36,400	8.70	3,166.80
June	39,000	9.00	3,510.00	35,000	8.50	2,975.00
July	41,000	9.25	3,792.50	34,000	8.25	2,805.00
August	52,000	9.25	4,810.00	31,500	8.25	2,598.75
September	50,500	9.00	4,545.00	31,400	8.00	2,512.00
October	40,000	9.40	3,760.00	35,700	7.50	2,677.50
November	39,500	9.50	3,752.50	32,100	8.00	2,568.00
December	38,500	9.50	3,657.50	31,400	8.00	2,512.00
Total monthly balances	$546,900	8.92%	$48,774.00	$467,500	8.47%	$39,603.80
Average monthly balance	42,069[a]			35,962[a]		

TABLE 12—Continued

Period	1972 Balance	1972 Rate	1972 Interest	1973 Balance	1973 Rate	1973 Interest
December						
(prior year)	$ 31,400	8.00%	$ 2,512.00	$ —	%	$ —
January	31,100	8.50	2,643.50	—		—
February	32,500	8.50	2,762.50	10,000	9.75	975.00
March	29,000	8.70	2,523.00	—		—
April	29,000	8.75	2,537.50	12,000	9.70	1,164.00
May	28,000	8.75	2,450.00	21,000	9.50	1,995.00
June	20,500	9.00	1,845.00	27,000	9.50	2,565.00
July	21,000	9.25	1,942.50	15,000	9.00	1,350.00
August	24,000	9.25	2,220.00	7,000	9.00	630.00
September	15,000	9.35	1,402.50	8,500	9.25	786.25
October	12,000	9.50	1,140.00	—		—
November	—		—	14,000	9.00	1,260.00
December	—		—	14,000	9.00	1,260.00
Total monthly balances	$273,500	8.77%	$23,978.50	$128,500	9.33%	$11,985.25
Average monthly balance	21,038ᵃ			9,885ᵃ		

NOTE: Similar calculations are performed for changes in working capital.
ᵃ Total monthly balance divided by 13.

deferred credits (income taxes and investment tax credits) are cost-free capital. Consequently, these do not require the determination of a reasonable cost rate.[55]

Column D of Table 13 illustrates the appropriate annual cost rate for each capital source. The cost rate for reinvested earnings and new issues of common stock is the commission's current allowed cost of equity capital. If there has not been a recent decision by the commission, the average actual return on equity capital for the latest three years is an acceptable alternative.[56] Depreciation is rated at the currently authorized rate of return. Since depreciation is derived from all previous investment sources of funds, the rate of return is the most appropriate to use. Deferred income taxes and deferred investment tax credits, being

---

[55] Although we have assumed all deferred credits to be tax free, a possible exception to this rule results from the Job Development Investment Tax Credit as enacted in the Revenue Act of 1971. Since the interest of Congress in passing the act was to

cost-free capital provided by rate payers, are given a "zero" rate. Long-term debt and preferred stock issues are rated at the cost for the new issues. The cost rate for notes payable is a weighted rate calculated for the year. The latter calculation is given on an annual basis in Table 12. Multiplying column D, the cost percentage, by column C, the percentage of weighted average dollars, provides the estimated weighted cost of money, by source, used for construction each year. This weighted cost should be used as a test of reasonableness of the overall AFC rate.

To provide for stability in the overall AFC rate in a particular year, a weighted average of the prior three years of construction fund sources is used. Tables 14A and 14B illustrate the weighting process. For example, the matrix of calculations for reinvested earnings for the 1970 line shows the weighted reinvested earnings of $6,920 for 1970 (from Table 9) and the actual 1970 year-end reinvested earnings of $9,200 for both 1971 and 1972 (from Table 12). In the latter two columns for 1970, the actual figures are appropriate since the actual funds were available throughout the years 1971 and 1972. For the year 1971, the matrix shows the weighted reinvested earnings of $3,318 for the 1971 line and the actual reinvested earnings for 1972. The 1972 line figure is the weighted amount of $3,946 for that year.

Similar matrixes are constructed for each of the other sources of funds (Tables 14A and 14B). Percentages of the totals for each source matrix

---

provide a sharing of benefits between consumer and investor, investment tax credits have a cost attached to them. To assure the sharing, the act prohibits (with some exceptions) a reduction in rate base or cost of service as a result of the credit utilization. Therefore, the unamortized credit balance must be included as part of the utility's total capitalization at a rate equal to either the company's overall rate of return or the cost of common equity. While no final methodology has been established as to the calculation of the correct rate, the two rates suggested have come from proposed rulemakings by the IRS and the Senate Finance Committee. As regards the investment tax credit on AFC, the weighted cost of funds used for construction, as illustrated in Table 6, would have to reflect the cost of the credit. 26 U.S.C.A. 46 (c), (e); *Revenue Act of 1971*, Senate Finance Committee General Explanation, Act Sec. 105 5005; and *Federal Register* 37 (17 February 1972): 3511–12 and 3526–30.

[56] The recent proposed rulemaking by the FPC also is suggesting this practice. FPC Docket No. RM75-27, Proposed Rulemaking "Uniform Systems of Accounts for Public Utilities Funds Used During Construction and Revisions of Certain Schedule Pages of FPC Reports," 20 May 1975, *Federal Register* 40 (29 May 1975): 23322.

TABLE 13. Estimated Cost of Money Used for Construction, 1970–1973

Sources of funds	Actual dollars[a] (A)	Weighted average dollars[b] (B)	Percentage of weighted average dollars[c] (C)	Cost (percentage) (D)	Weighted cost (E)
1970					
Reinvested earnings (net income less dividends paid)	9,200	6,920	8.4	10.50[d]	0.882
Depreciation	21,000	10,292	12.4	7.15[e]	0.887
Deferred income tax	1,900	607	0.7	—[f]	—
Deferred investment tax credit	2,000	1,042	1.3	—[f]	—
Long-term debt	40,000	21,923	26.5	7.50[g]	1.988
Common stock	—	—	—	—	—
Preferred stock	—	—	—	—	—
Notes payable	—	42,069	50.7	8.92[h]	4.522
		82,853	100.0		8.279
1971					
Reinvested earnings	4,500	3,318	3.9	10.50[d]	.410
Depreciation	23,500	11,673	13.7	7.15[e]	.980
Deferred income tax	3,300	1,247	1.5	—[f]	—
Deferred investment tax credit	600	297	0.3	—[f]	—
Long-term debt	50,000	32,692	38.4	7.95[g]	3.052
Common stock	—	—	—	—	—
Preferred stock	—	—	—	—	—
Notes payable	—	35,962	42.2	8.47[h]	3.574
		85,189	100.0		8.016

1972					
Reinvested earnings	10,300	3,946	6.2	10.50[d]	0.651
Depreciation	26,000	12,621	19.8	7.15[e]	1.416
Deferred income tax	5,700	2,873	4.5	—[f]	—
Deferred investment tax credit	3,100	1,342	2.1	—[f]	—
Long-term debt	50,000	13,462	21.1	8.75[g]	1.846
Common stock	29,000	8,371	13.2	10.50[d]	1.386
Preferred stock	—	—	—	—	—
Notes payable		21,038	33.1	8.77[h]	2.903
		63,653	100.0		8.202

1973					
Reinvested earnings	16,300	6,571	10.0	10.50[d]	1.050
Depreciation	28,400	14,562	22.2	7.15[e]	1.587
Deferred income tax	5,600	2,919	4.5	—	—
Deferred investment tax credit	1,300	523	0.8	—	—
Long-term debt	—	—	—	—	—
Common stock	36,600	5,630	8.6	10.50[d]	0.903
Preferred stock	30,000	25,385	38.8	8.95[g]	3.473
Notes payable		9,885	15.1	9.33[h]	1.409
		65,475	100.0		8.422

[a] From Table 8.
[b] From Tables 9, 10, 11, and 12.
[c] Weighted average source of construction funds (each source) for column B, divided by total weighted source (column B).
[d] Latest commission authorized cost of common equity.
[e] Latest commission authorized rate of return.
[f] Cost-free capital.
[g] Cost of new issue.
[h] See Table 12 for rate calculations.

TABLE 14A. Estimated AFC Rate and Cost of Construction Funds, 1973

Source		Overall AFC rate for 1973						
		1970	1971	1972	Total	Percent-age of total	Percent-age of cost	Weighted cost
				(dollars)				
Reinvested earnings	1970	6920	9200	9200	25320			
	1971		3318	4500	7818			
	1972			3946	3946			
		6920	12518	17646	37084	8.0	10.50	0.840
Depreciation	1970	10292	21000	21000	52292			
	1971		11673	23500	35173			
	1972			12621	12621			
		10292	32673	57121	100086	21.7	7.15	1.552
Deferred income tax and deferred investment tax credit	1970	1649	3900	3900	9449			
	1971		1544	3900	5444			
	1972			4215	4215			
		1649	5444	12015	19108	4.1	—	—
Long-term debt	1970	21923	40000	40000	101923	22.0	7.50	1.650
	1971		32692	50000	82692	18.0	7.95	1.431
	1972			13462	13462	2.9	8.75	0.254
		21923	72692	103462	198077	42.9		
Common stock	1970	—	—	—	—			
	1971		—	—	—			
	1972			8371	8371			
		—	—	8371	8371	1.8	10.50	0.189

Preferred stock							
1970	—	—	—	—	—	—	—
1971	—	—	—	—	—	—	0.812
1972	—	—	—	—	—	—	0.661
	—	—	—	—	—	—	0.403
Notes payable							
1970	42069	—	—	42069	9.1	8.92	0.812
1971	—	35962	—	35962	7.8	8.47	0.661
1972	—	—	21038	21038	4.6	8.77	0.403
	42069	35962	21038	99069	21.5		7.792
				461795	100.0		

TABLE 14B. Estimated AFC Rate and Cost of Construction Funds, 1974

Source		1971	1972	1973	Total	Percentage of total	Percentage of cost	Weighted cost
			(dollars)					
Reinvested earnings	1971	3318	4500	4500	12318			
	1972		3946	10300	14246			
	1973			6571	6571			
		3318	8446	21371	33135	6.6	10.50	0.693
Depreciation	1971	11673	23500	23500	58673			
	1972		12621	26000	38621			
	1973			14562	14562			
		11673	36121	64062	111856	22.3	7.15	1.594
Deferred income tax and deferred investment tax credit	1971	1544	3900	3900	9344			
	1972		4215	8800	13015			
	1973			3442	3442			
		1544	8115	16142	25801	5.1	—	—
Long-term debt	1971	32692	50000	50000	132692	26.4	7.95	2.099
	1972		13462	50000	63462	12.6	8.75	1.103
	1973			—	—			
		32692	63462	100000	196154	39.0		
Common stock	1971	—	—	—	—			
	1972		8371	29000	37371			
	1973			5630	5630			
		—	8371	34630	43001	8.6	10.50	0.903

	1971	1972	1973	Total	%	Cost rate	Weighted cost
Preferred stock							
1971	—	—					
1972	—	—					
1973			25385	25385	5.1	8.95	0.456
			25385	25385			
Notes payable							
1971	35962	—	—	35962	7.1	8.47	0.601
1972	—	21038	—	21038	4.2	8.77	0.368
1973	—	—	9885	9885	2.0	9.33	0.187
	35962	21038	9885	66885	13.3		
				502217	100.0		8.004

are calculated. These percentages are then multiplied by their respective percentage costs (from Table 13, column D) to arrive at the fund component weighted cost. A summation of these weighted costs provides the overall AFC rate to be used for the particular year. Thus, the rate for 1973 is 7.792 percent.

The weighting process not only helps to stabilize the overall AFC rate over time, but also puts short-term financing into proper perspective. If the weighting process were not used, the short-term funds would have too great an impact on the overall rate. Obversely, the weighting recognizes more appropriately the proper role of permanent financing, which without such weighting could be underrepresented since this financing is often done in the latter part of the year.

The result of weighting the calculations also produces a conservative overall AFC rate, somewhat less than the calculated cost of money (Table 13), yet recognizes all major sources of funds and their attendant costs.

While this example uses a three-year average, other periods may be more appropriate to the individual utility, depending upon the average time required to complete construction projects.

The weighted average rate then is applied to average monthly balances in the construction work in progress account to determine the dollar amount of AFC capitalized monthly.[57]

---

[57] Other alternative methods have been utilized or suggested for calculating an acceptable overall AFC rate. For example, the New York Public Service Commission has a suggested methodology for rate determination to be used by public utilities under their jurisdiction (Subject Memorandum: "Rate at which to capitalize interest during construction," 24 October 1972). This methodology, as given in the memo, says:

> If, for example, a utility is capitalized with 55 percent long-term debt at 6 percent, 10 percent preferred stock at 7.5 percent, and 35 percent common stock, and if in the last rate case a return of 12 percent on common equity was found to be reasonable, and if the utility is financing construction projects 60 percent from permanent financings and 40 percent from short-term borrowings at 5.5 percent, the interest rate employed in capitalizing interest during construction should approximate:

> 60 percent × 55 percent × 6   percent = 1.98
> 60 percent × 10 percent × 7.5 percent = 0.45
> 60 percent × 35 percent × 12.0 percent = 2.52
> 40 percent ×   × 5.5 percent = 2.20
>   ‾‾‾‾‾‾‾‾‾‾‾‾‾
>   7.15 percent

(footnote 57 continued)

In most instances, this approach should yield a rate for capitalizing interest during construction at less than the overall rate of return allowed in the preceding rate case, and, in all likelihood, lower than the overall rate of return which would be permitted in a subsequent rate case.

Another approach has been suggested by Robert E. Frazer and Richard C. Ranson of Duke Power Company. In their article, "Is Interest During Construction 'Funny Money'?" (*Public Utilities Fortnightly* 90 [21 December 1972]: 21–22), they state:

Normally (the sources) will consist of funds generated from depreciation, long- and short-term borrowings, preferred and common stock, as well as earnings retained in the business and used to finance construction. Quite often average short-term borrowings will be a significant component of the capital underlying the construction program. Thus, it is important to include the average short-term debt and its related cost in arriving at an IDC rate.

Below is an example of a logical method of arriving at a rate for IDC. To simplify the illustration, cash flow from depreciation has been omitted. The reader will note that the gross rate of 9.56 percent has been reduced for the income tax deduction related to the interest on bonds and short-term debt, assuming a tax rate of 50 percent, so that the net IDC rate is 7.31 percent.

ILLUSTRATION 3

	Average Capital- ization Ratios	Average Construc- tion Work in Progress		Current Rate	IDC Rate
Bonds	55%	$ 96	48%	8%	3.84%
Preferred	10	18	9	8	.72
Common Equity	35	61	31	14	4.34
	100%	$175			
Average Short-term Debt Used in Construction		25	12	5½	.66
Average CWIP		$200	100%		9.56%
Income Tax (3.84% + .66%)= 4.50% × 50% = 2.25%					2.25
Net IDC rate					7.31%

(footnote 57 continued)

Current Cash Portion:

Bonds	3.84%
Preferred	.72
Short-term Debt	.66
Taxes	(2.25)
	2.97%

Current Cash: 2.97% ÷ 7.31% = 41%
Noncash: Equity Component = 59
100%

Note that Frazer and Ranson in their debt component calculation have utilized a net of tax approach, while the New York Public Service Commission method and our method have applied a before tax approach. The reason for the difference stems from a difference in perspective. Apparently, Frazer and Ranson view the overall AFC rate as being based upon a cost to the utility, whereas our formula and that of the New York Commission view the overall AFC rate as a compensation to the lender for the use of his funds. If one regards the debt component of AFC as an offset to interest expense, then one should use a before tax approach in order to eliminate all of the interest expense associated with construction. (Note this is consistent with FPC rulemaking RM75-27, *Federal Register* 40 [29 May 1975]: 23323.)

Depending upon the point of view, either approach (that is, net of tax or before tax) has merit, and either concept is applicable to all three methods, although we favor the before tax approach since the calculation before taxes is consistent with the use of tax allocation procedures advocated by the FPC (*Order No. 530*, issued 18 June 1975) and with the new proposed rulemaking RM75-27 described below.

The most recent suggestion to come forth for the determination of an acceptable AFC rate has been that of the FPC in its proposed rulemaking RM75-27. The proposal involves a formulation to be incorporated in Electric Plant Instructions (17) of the uniform system of accounts by adding three new paragraphs, (a), (b), and (c), as follows (Docket No. RM75-27, *Federal Register* 40 [29 May 1975]: 23323):

Electric Plant Instructions

*   *   *   *   *

3. Components of Construction Cost.

*   *   *   *   *

(17) "Allowance for funds used during construction" includes the net cost for the period of construction of borrowed funds used for construction purposes and a reasonable rate on other funds when so used, not to exceed allowances computed in accordance with the formula

(footnote 57 continued)

prescribed in paragraph (a) below. No allowance for funds used during construction charges shall be included in these accounts upon expenditures for construction projects which have been abandoned.

(a) The formula and elements for the computation of the allowance for funds used during construction shall be:

$$A_i = s \left(\frac{S}{W} \right) + d \left(\frac{D}{D+P+C} \right) \left(1 - \frac{S}{W} \right)$$

$$A_e = \left[1 - \frac{S}{W} \right] \left[p \left(\frac{P}{D+P+C} \right) + c \left(\frac{C}{D+P+C} \right) \right]$$

A_i = Allowance for borrowed funds used during construction rate.
A_e = Allowance for other funds used during construction rate.
S = Average short-term debt.
s = Short-term debt interest rate.
D = Average long-term debt.
d = Long-term debt interest rate.
P = Average preferred stock.
p = Preferred stock cost rate.
C = Average common equity.
c = Common equity cost rate.
W = Average construction work in progress balance.

(b) The rates shall be determined annually and the various components in the formula for the current year rates shall be derived from actual book balances and book cost rates for the prior year, with the exception that the rate used for common equity shall be the rate granted common equity in the last rate proceeding before the rate-making body having primary rate jurisdiction. If such rate is not available, the average rate actually earned during the preceding three years shall be used.

(c) For those companies which are required to flow-through the interest expense portion of AFUDC in computing income taxes for cost of service purposes, the utility would use the gross AFUDC rate. For companies where the interest portion of AFUDC is not utilized in computing income taxes for cost of service purposes, depending upon the requirements of the appropriate regulatory commission, a net-of-tax rate should be used or a gross rate with appropriate normalization entries for the tax effect of the interest.

As regards the application of our method over the New York, Frazer-Ranson, or proposed FPC methods, we feel that our technique provides a better measurement of the true, overall AFC rate and better meets the criteria which were set forth above as being desirable.

6

The Effects and
Significance of AFC

One significant reason for the concern regarding accounting for allowance for funds used during construction is the impact that it can have on the financial picture of an electric utility. This impact is due in large part to the sanction, in the uniform system of accounts, which allows these utilities to capitalize AFC on *all* funds used for construction, thus recognizing not only actual but also imputed costs in the financial records. Some of the reasons for capitalizing AFC were discussed earlier,[1] but actual accounting for these costs was not described in detail. The purpose of this chapter is to provide an analysis and evaluation of the actual accounting used by electric utilities. The discussion will be presented, in part, within a theoretical framework to determine whether accounting for AFC is consistent with sound accounting theory and principles. In addition, an evaluation of the impact which the present accounting for these funds has on the utility's financial statements is presented. The chapter concludes with a discussion of certain income tax implications resulting from the capitalization of AFC.

---

[1] See chapter 5, pp. 65–66.

ACCOUNTING FOR THE AFC CREDIT

Electric utilities account for AFC as prescribed by the various uniform systems of accounts. These firms, for the most part, are subject to either the FPC or the NARUC systems of accounts, both of which are virtually identical in their prescriptions. The ensuing discussion will illustrate the effects of prescribed accounting for AFC on the various financial statements.

AFC and the Balance Sheet

Under the FPC and NARUC systems of accounts, utilities that capitalize AFC debit the account "Construction work in progress" for the full amount of allowance capitalized. When the project is placed in service, the "Construction work in progress" account then is cleared to a "Utility plant" account, and at that point the amount transferred can become part of the utility's rate base. Although the debit to the accounts for AFC capitalized contains an imputed amount representing an allowance capitalized on the utility's other funds, this imputed amount always has been considered a necessary component of construction cost; thus, the debit has been subject to little or no controversy. Exhibit 3 illustrates the plant section of the utility balance sheet containing the accounts used.

EXHIBIT 3.   ABC Utility, Partial Balance Sheet,
31 December 19_____

Assets and Other Debits

Utility Plant

Utility plant in service[a]	xxx
Less: Accumulated provision for depreciation	xxx
Net utility plant in service	xxxx
Utility plant leased to others	xxx
Construction work in progress[b]	xxx
Utility plant acquisition adjustments	xxx
Total net utility plant	xxxx

[a] When plant is placed in service, construction work in progress generally is cleared to this account.
[b] Initial debit for allowance for funds used during construction goes into this account.

AFC and the Income Statement

Under the FPC and NARUC systems the amount of all AFC capitalized is credited on the income statement. Until 1971 both systems classified this credit as a deduction in the interest charges section in the account "Interest charged to construction—cr."[2] In August 1971, however, the FPC issued *Order No. 436*, which altered both the title and the classification of the account on the income statement.[3] The title was changed from "Interest charged to construction—cr." to "Allowance for funds used during construction," and the account was moved from the "Interest charges" section to the "Other income" section of the income statement.[4] The NARUC system's 1972 revisions made identical changes. Exhibit 4 illustrates the AFC credit in the income statement prior to 1971–1972 and currently. Although there is a difference in classification under the older and newer systems, the net effect of these credits within the respective systems is the same.[5] Both create the unique situation whereby a utility, by capitalizing AFC, can affect the net income of the enterprise.[6] As shown in Exhibit 4, the imputed portion of the AFC charge, attributable to the utility's other funds, is credited to other *income*, whereas the credit for the capitalization of actual interest paid on borrowed funds is in effect an offset to interest

---

[2] NARUC, *Uniform System*, p. 113; and FPC, *Uniform System*, p. 68.

[3] FPC, "Order Amending the Uniform System of Accounts for Class A and B Public Utilities and Licensees and Natural Gas Companies and Certain FPC Report Forms, Concerning Interest Charged to Construction," *Order No. 436* (Washington, D.C.: the Commission, 9 August 1971), pp. 4–5.

[4] Ibid., but in the most recent FPC proposed rulemaking, RM75-27, the FPC is suggesting a breakdown of AFC into two components—borrowed funds and other funds. Under "Other income" would be included an account, "Allowance for other funds during construction." Under the caption "Interest charges" would be added a new account, "Allowance for borrowed funds used during construction." *Federal Register* 40 (29 May 1975): 73331.

[5] The older method is being illustrated since some state commissions still use the 1958 version of the NARUC system.

[6] A modification to the above income statement reporting was suggested at a recent public utility conference held at Iowa State University. Mr. William J. Powell, Chief, Division of Systems Office of Accounting and Finance, Federal Power Commission, suggested that the allowance for funds used for construction be identified by debt and other (equity) sources and that the allowance on the debt portion be excluded from the income statement; if it must be shown, it should be done with a short column showing full interest expense with the AFC portion be-

expense, thus having no net income effect.[7] Since the imputed portion, which also is credited, has no corresponding debit in the income statement, net income is increased by the amount of that credit. The necessity for utilities to capitalize an imputed allowance on other funds if they wish to recover the capital costs of these funds in the future has been discussed previously.[8] The issue at this point is the propriety, under regulatory principles and accounting theory, of including this portion of the credit as income in the income statement.[9]

A number of aspects must be investigated. Is it essential to credit income for this imputed amount from the practical and theoretical viewpoints of regulation? If so, is there any support for this practice in economic and accounting theory? Answers to these questions can aid in determining not only the validity of the practice, but also, if it is not valid, any possible alternatives.

From a regulatory standpoint, the credit on the income statement representing the imputed portion of capitalized AFC is viewed in an economic sense as a means of offsetting the foregone opportunity for

---

ing deducted therefrom. His rationale was that interest on debt is not different from other capitalized expenses, such as overheads, which are not first shown in the income statement as expenses and later as income. The same should hold true for interest expense on debt. Regarding the allowance on equity funds, however, Powell feels that this portion of AFC must be shown because value was added to the construction project. Even though it is not a cash flow, the value is a true one to be recoverable in future utility rates. "Pertaining to Calculation and Reporting of the Allowance for Funds Used During Construction (ADC)," paper presented at the Iowa State Conference on Public Utility Rates, Ames, Iowa, 15–17 May 1973.

[7] This would be true if comparing reported net income when the utility borrowed funds specifically to finance construction and interest was capitalized, and reported net income when the utility had not undertaken the construction project and not borrowed the funds. Everett Morris, "Capitalization of Interest on Construction: Time for Reappraisal?" *Public Utilities Fortnightly* 75 (4 March 1971): 22–23.

[8] See chapter 5, pp. 65–66.

[9] Although the imputed portion of the credit has been reported for many years as income on the financial statements to regulatory authorities, it should be pointed out that the FPC has assumed authority over utilities under its jurisdiction in the area of financial reporting to the public as well. Reports to stockholders must conform to the accounting requirements as set forth under the uniform system of accounts. See *Appalachian Power Company* v. *Federal Power Commission*, 328 F. 2d 237 (4th Cir. 1964).

EXHIBIT 4. ABC Utility, Partial Income Statement for Year Ended 31 December 19_____		
	FPC and NARUC Systems	
	Before 1971–1972	*Currently*
Net utility operating income	xxxx	xxxx
Other Income and Deductions		
Other income:		
Nonutility operating income	xxx	xxx
Interest and dividend income	xxx	xxx
Allowance for funds used during construction		xxx
Total other income	xxxx	xxxx
Total income	xxxx	xxxx
Miscellaneous income deductions	xxx	xxx
Income before interest charges	xxxx	xxxx
Interest charges:		
Interest on long-term debt	xxx	xxx
Amortization of debt discount, premium, and expense	xxx	xxx
Other interest expense	xxx	xxx
Interest charged to construction—cr.	(xxx)	
Total interest charges	xxxx	xxxx
Income before extraordinary charges	xxxx	xxxx

the investors to earn a return on the company's own funds utilized for the purpose of construction.[10] The additional income created by this credit is comparable to a return on the new plant when it is placed in service. From this perspective, if a utility did not credit income for the imputed amount, reported net income during the construction period could be depressed to the point of discouraging future investment. This could result in the inability of utilities to construct additional assets required to meet the needs of their customers.[11] Crediting income with this amount allows utility income and earnings per share to remain relatively unchanged between the periods of construction and operations, eliminating the possible need for rate adjustments during that

---

[10] Arthur Andersen and Co., *Principles*, p. 27; chapter 2.
[11] Richard Walker, "Interest During Construction Credits," paper presented to the New York Society of Security Analysts, New York, 30 November 1970, p. 10.

time. Thus, from an economic or regulatory standpoint, there seems to be sound reasoning to support crediting income for the imputed amount of AFC.

Whether or not crediting income for the imputed amount of AFC can be justified as a sound accounting practice involves considerations very different from those presented with regard to the economic regulatory practice. When an investor examines the income statement of a utility and sees an item listed as income, he should be able to assume that from an accounting viewpoint, it is in fact income.

Under the present accounting systems, the imputed amount of capitalized AFC credited to income infers that a utility can derive income through the construction of assets, despite the generally accepted accounting principle that income should not be recorded until it is recognized, and that it normally is not recognized until realization has occurred. The fundamental question is whether there is any basis under sound accounting theory for this treatment of imputed cost by the utility.

A review of the accounting literature reveals that several individuals have claimed that there is no theoretical basis for recognizing any imputed amount as income in the utility situation.[12] These accountants contend that any credits arising from the capitalization of this imputed cost are in the nature of permanent capital rather than income and thus should be reflected as such on the balance sheet. In part, their reasoning is based on the idea that these credits do not of themselves generate cash for dividend payments, since cash derived from these credits to fund the payment of dividends materializes only through revenue requirements recovered over the life of the asset.[13] Thus, this group views the nature of the transaction, which increases the cost of an asset

---

[12] See, for example, W. C. Reyer, "Accounting for Construction in Public Utilities," *Journal of Accountancy* 32 (September 1921): 191; American Institute of Accountants, Library and Bureau of Information, "Interest Charged to Construction," *Special Bulletin No. 27* (New York: the Institute, December 1926), p. 7; John H. Bickley, "Interest During Construction in Public Utility Accounting," *Journal of Land and Public Utility Economics* 1 (October 1925): 417; and William A. Paton, ed., *Accountant's Handbook*, 2d ed. (New York: Ronald Press, 1939), p. 810.

[13] Ralph F. Gates, "Interest During Construction," paper presented to an accounting workshop at the National Association of Regulatory and Utility commissioners' convention, Philadelphia, Pennsylvania, 12 October 1959, p. 2.

through an imputed amount, as only giving rise to additional investment. Consequently, they contend that the credit should be reflected
as an item of paid-in or capital surplus.

The inference in the above argument is that the AFC credit should
not go to income because it would be transferred to retained earnings,
making it available for dividends. Although true, this argument alone
is not a valid reason for recording the credit to permanent capital. The
present absence of cash to pay dividends does not make an item part of
permanent investment. If the sole purpose for keeping this credit out of
income is to preclude the payment of dividends, then all that need be
done is to restrict retained earnings for the amount of the credit.

Those who contend that the credit should be made to paid-in or capital surplus do not present strong theoretical support. Examining the
sources from which paid-in or capital surplus normally is derived appears to negate the claim that the imputed AFC credit is an element of
permanent capital. Generally, paid-in or capital surplus is derived from
(1) transactions in the company's own stock; (2) stockholders' contributions; (3) contributions by outsiders, including gifts of assets and for-
giveness of indebtedness; and (4) distributions of stock dividends and
similar actions ordered by the board of directors by which some portion
of retained earnings is reclassified as part of the capital of the corporation
and thus credited to the capital stock and paid-in surplus accounts.[14] The
point is that the imputed AFC credit does not arise as a result of the
above characteristic transactions and should not be classified as a part
of permanent investment.

A second group of accountants claims that the present practice of
crediting income for the capitalized imputed amount of AFC is perfectly proper in the utility situation. Their reasoning is based on a dual
premise: (1) In the unique utility situation, the need arises to capitalize
an imputed amount of interest on the company's other funds; thus, this
amount is a legitimate cost; and (2) there is reasonable expectation that
this cost can be collected over the life of the asset. Thus, proponents
maintain that, in effect, the imputed amount is similar in nature to a
receivable whose collectibility is extended over the useful life of the
asset. With a reasonable assurance that the utility, which has the right
to earn a return but is not guaranteed a return, successfully can recover
its investment, there is every justification for recognizing this credit in

---

[14] Finney and Miller, *Principles*, p. 104.

income while the asset is being constructed.[15] This group draws an analogy from the accounting concept that a sale is recorded as revenue at the point when collectibility reasonably is assured. Similarly, in the utility case they contend that realization of income should take place at the time of capitalization, for this is when the collectibility of this imputed amount is reasonably established.

A third proposal, which is a modification of the second, has been advanced. The basic premise is that revenue should not be recognized by constructing assets; thus, any income should be deferred and not recognized until the asset is actually in service and producing revenue. It is suggested that a deferred credit be established for the imputed amount of interest, with subsequent periodic recognition of income as the asset is depreciated.[16] The effect is to delay recognition of this income to the periods of operation. It should be noted that proponents of the second proposal also would advocate delaying recognition through a deferred credit when a utility has not yet proven its ability to recover its investment and earn a fair rate of return. This group, however, probably would make a retroactive adjustment to income, thus recognizing the credit as such once the utility has proven itself.[17]

In assessing the relative merits of the last two proposals, it becomes fairly obvious that the uniqueness of the utility situation, which necessitates the recognition of an imputed amount in the accounts, requires that any accounting conclusion also must consider the regulatory environment within which the utility operates. This, of course, does not mean that accounting theory might not be helpful in determining which of the two alternatives is most appropriate in the utility situation. As was discussed in chapter 3, existing accounting concepts preclude the inclusion of imputed costs in the accounts of unregulated industrial and commercial enterprises, but in that context there is no need for imputing costs, as there is in the utility case. By assuming, however, that such a need did exist in the nonutility sector, the theoretical issues of accounting for imputed costs discussed with reference to that sector might

---

[15] Walker, "Interest During Construction Credits," p. 8.

[16] Bierman, *Financial Accounting*, pp. 59–60.

[17] The private records of various accounting firms indicate that such a procedure had been adopted in certain cases of new utilities which had not yet proven their ability to recover their investment. New utilities are not very common today, however.

aid in determining the accounting nature of the credit as it relates to the unique utility situation. Although there appears to be little evidence to support the contention that this necessary imputed cost incurred by utilities is an item of permanent capital, an essential question still remains: Is there a basis in accounting theory for recognizing such cost as realized income at the time it is capitalized, or does income realization occur sometime after construction, which implies that the recognition of income should be delayed? This question requires more thorough examination of the realization concept.

The matter of when income is realized long has been subject to different meanings and interpretations. Traditionally, the term *realization* has meant the recognition of revenue or income at the time an exchange occurs. This narrow view has necessitated certain exceptions. As succinctly stated by Blough, "while it is generally understood that income should be recognized when services are rendered or goods delivered, in practice the time of taking it up ranges all the way from the time of production, as in the case of some mining enterprises, to the time cash is received, as is sometimes done in the case of installment sales."[18] If there is no single rule to be applied in all situations, the proper solution seems to lie in the careful consideration of all facts surrounding the circumstances of each case.

Some of the traditional criteria set forth by accountants for realization cannot be applied readily to the problem at hand. For example, Paton and Littleton say that realization is met by two tests: (1) conversion through legal sale or similar process, and (2) validation through the acquisition of liquid assets.[19] Similarly, the American Accounting Association Concepts and Standards Research Study Committee, in its report on the realization concept, states that realization takes place in a revenue transaction when (1) the asset received in a revenue transaction is measurable, (2) the accounting entity is party to a market transaction, and (3) the crucial event in the revenue process has occurred.[20] The Accounting Principles Board of the AICPA defines realization as follows: "Realization. Revenue is generally recognized when both of the following conditions are met: (1) the earning process is complete or virtually

---

[18] Carman G. Blough, "Challenges to the Accounting Profession in the United States," *Journal of Accountancy* 108 (December 1959): 39.

[19] Paton and Littleton, *Corporate Accounting*, p. 49.

[20] AAA, "The Realization Concept," pp. 314–18.

complete and (2) an exchange has taken place."[21] While implicit in these statements are certain standards, such as a legal sale, receipt of an asset, completion of an earning process, or a market transaction, none presents the unique case of imputing AFC, which in the utility situation normally is recognized as realized income. Apparently, any support for recognizing the imputed credit as realized income at the time the interest is capitalized cannot be found by examining the traditional attitudes toward realization.

In 1957 the American Accounting Association Committee on Concepts and Standards Underlying Corporate Financial Statements set forth a broad definition of realization which differed from the traditional views.

> The essential meaning of realization is that a change in an asset or liability has become sufficiently definite and objective to warrant recognition in the accounts. This recognition may rest on an exchange transaction between independent parties, or on established trade practices, or on the terms of a contract performance of which is considered to be virtually certain. It may depend on the stability of a banking system, the enforceability of commercial agreements or the ability of a highly organized market to facilitate the conversion of an asset into another form.[22]

This definition differs from tradition by stating that realization takes place when, as a result of an exchange transaction, a positive contractual commitment, or established trade practice, a measurable and objectively determinable increase in an asset occurs. Floyd Windal, in applying this broader definition to the specific case of income or revenue realization, sets forth the following criteria:

1. The monetary amount of the revenue or income can be definitely determined or can be estimated with a reasonable degree of accuracy.

2. One of the following is true:
   a. An exchange transaction has taken place with an independent outside party and
      (1) Cash or marketable securities have been received in the amount of the increase or
      (2) In the accountant's judgment, the completion of the transaction is virtually certain.

---

[21] APB, *Statement No. 4*, p. 59.
[22] AAA, "The Realization Concept," p. 3.

    b. A contract or commercial agreement has been entered into, and the service related to that contract or agreement has been utilized.

    c. The enterprise has been legally relieved of some of its liabilities.

    d. In the accountant's judgment, it is a virtual impossibility that an asset increase will be reversed.[23]

Assessing the applicability of these criteria to the issue of viewing the imputed credit as income in the utility situation again requres an examination of the reason for capitalizing AFC, which always has been considered a legitimate cost of construction. Recording this cost is a recognition that the utility must have the opportunity to recover all costs of service. Under the regulatory framework this is accomplished by booking these costs in the plant accounts. Notwithstanding the facts that by so doing gross assets are increased and that AFC is capable of being measured objectively, it appears that none of the criteria in item (2) above is satisfied. Thus, there is no apparent basis for using this broader definition to equate realization with the mere capitalization of an imputed allowance when applied to utilities. From the viewpoint of sound accounting theory, it seems the credit arising from capitalizing imputed interest should be deferred, and the income should be recognized as it is realized over the life of the property, to the extent that revenues cover depreciation charges. There is little if any theoretical justification for recognizing the imputed credit as realized income at the time the allowance is capitalized.

Although this practice does not appear to be sound from an accounting theory viewpoint, the unique circumstance of rate regulation, to which the utility is subject,[24] creates a special need for recognizing this credit as current income.

AFC and the Funds Statement

As part of the ever increasing demands for relevant accounting data, in 1970 the FPC issued *Order No. 416* amending the FPC Annual Report Form No. 1; two new schedule pages (numbers 118 and 119) were

---

[23] Floyd W. Windal, "The Accounting Concept of Realization," *Accounting Review* 36 (April 1961): 256.

[24] See chapter 1.

added: Statement E—Sources and Application of Funds for the Year 19____.[25] This action conformed with the earlier pronouncements of the AICPA and its requirements for the funds statement.[26]

The FPC explained this new requirement for funds flow data as necessary to meet the demands by the users of utility financial resources —cash and near cash items—which may be used to acquire other assets and discharge obligations. The income statement and balance sheet alone are insufficient in measuring the health of a firm because they fail to recognize fund flows; the funds statement fills this gap. The statement is particularly relevant for the present discussion in that it provides data of funds used in construction projects for the period analyzed. In fact, a popular modification describes all funds used for construction.[27] Also indicated are the AFC funds capitalized for the same period.

Exhibit 5 illustrates a sample funds statement. The required statement displays funds derived from operations, or net income, noncash outlays including allowance for funds used during construction, and funds derived from outside financing. With regard to the noncash outlays and the AFC component in particular, the FPC stated in *Accounting Release No. AR-10*: "When reporting the Source of Funds the amounts relating to 'interest during construction' should be reported as an item under 'Other (net):' line 8, 'Principal Non-Cash Charges (Credits) to Income:'. When reporting the Application of Funds, each item under the Construction and Plant Expenditures (inc. land) section shall be reduced by the related amount of 'interest during construction' added thereto during the period."[28]

While it has been established that AFC is a legitimate construction cost, it is also a fact that, as a noncash source of funds, AFC does not provide a current cash flow. At least it seems reasonable to assume that the imputed allowance on equity capital is in this category. Yet, one also might argue that all AFC, regardless of source, eventually will be charged against operations through depreciation. Since depreciation is added in full to the net income in determining sources of funds from

25 Federal Power Commission, Docket No. R-396, *Order No. 416*, 7 December 1970 (18-CFR 141.1, 260.1).

26 AICPA, *Opinions of the Accounting Principles Board*, No. 3 and No. 19 (New York: the Institute, 1963; 1971).

27 See chapter 5, p. 95.

28 FPC, *Accounting Release No. AR-10* (Washington, D.C.: the Commission, 11 January 1971).

EXHIBIT 5. ABC Utility, Sources and Application of Funds for Year Ending 31 December 19_____			
Sources of Funds			
Funds from internal sources:	xxx		
Funds from operations			
Principle noncash outlays:			
Depreciation and amortization	xxx		
Deferred taxes and deferred investment credits	xxx		
Allowance for funds used during construction[a]	(xxx)		
Total funds from internal sources		xxx	
Funds from outside sources:			
Long-term debt	xxx		
Preferred stock	xxx		
Common stock	xxx		
Net decrease in working capital	xxx		
Total funds from outside sources		xxx	
Total sources of funds			xxxx
Application of Funds			
Construction and plant expenditures[b]	xxx		
Dividends on preferred stock	xxx		
Dividends on common stock	xxx		
Retirement of securities	xxx		
Total application of funds			xxxx

[a] Location on statement established by Federal Power Commission in *Accounting Release AR-10*, 11 January 1971.
[b] Less allowance for funds used during construction.

operations, it is likely that the sources of funds could be overstated if the full AFC amount were not deducted in determining sources of funds.[29] This reduction of the full AFC amount is in conformity with the FPC's *AR-10* quoted above.

IMPACT OF AFC ON
NET INCOME AND EARNINGS PER SHARE

It generally is considered acceptable for electric utilities capitalizing AFC to credit an account in the income statement for the full amount

---

[29] Lyle M. Dahlenburg, "Allowance for Funds Used During Construction—Calculation and Disclosure Problems," *Public Utilities Fortnightly* 93 (17 January 1974): 23.

capitalized, including an imputed amount for the utility's own funds. This practice always has been a complicating factor and a controversial one for investment and security analysts, who must analyze the effect of this credit on utility earnings. This group and others have expressed concern over the growing size of AFC credits because they do not give rise to present cash-flow earnings, but are merely claims to future revenues. Those portions of net income resulting from allowances are being challenged as inferior to income which results from operating revenues. For example, in chapter 1 several instances were cited in which investment analysts, accountants, and economists have expressed concern over the quality of earnings being affected by AFC.[30]

Although some of the challenges are quite valid and are difficult to dispute, the manner in which many have viewed these allowance credits indicates a misunderstanding as to their true nature. For example, utilities sometimes experience a decline in net income in the year following a period of heavy construction because of a hiatus before earnings from operations are sufficient to offset the loss of the AFC credit. There are two major reasons for insufficient initial operating earnings. First, after construction ceases on a generating plant, a further shakedown period still may be required. Second, at times a temporary excess capacity may exist which prevents a new plant from earning a full operating return.[31]

Because of the possible decline of earnings at this time, it is reported that many analysts, in comparing the earnings of these utilities, deduct the entire amount of the AFC credit.[32] Apparently they assume that if the AFC credit represents true earnings, then the utilities should not experience any income reduction after construction is completed. They are skeptical about the credits and believe that earnings from them should not be considered as such until they are recovered in future revenues.[33]

Those analysts who deduct the AFC credit fail to comprehend fully the purpose for the initial capitalization. First, by excluding the entire credit they overlook the fact that part of this amount represents interest

---

[30] See chapter 1, pp. 4–5.

[31] Ely Owen, "Interest Credit Versus Plant under Construction," *Public Utilities Fortnightly* 70 (16 August 1962): 232.

[32] Madigan, "Depreciation," p. 6.

[33] Goodbody and Co., *A Comparative Study of the Interest-During-Construction Credit for 108 Electric Utility Companies* (New York: the Company, 16 September 1963), p. 2.

incurred on borrowed funds, and this portion does not in any way affect the net income.[34] Second, and more important, the decline in earnings, as discussed above, is not due to a fault in the accounting practice of capitalizing AFC, but to a flaw in the regulatory process. If the new level of revenues generated after construction fails to provide a reasonable return on total investments, the decline occurs because the utility no longer can utilize the efficient practice of capitalization, but must rely on the commissions to prescribe rates which adequately will compensate them. In many cases, the regulatory process cannot react quickly enough, and a drop in earnings may ensue. Any solution to the problem is not to be found in ignoring the AFC credit, but in trying to improve the regulatory machinery so that it is more responsive to the needs of the utility.[35]

It is quite true that, in the last few years, the AFC credits continually have grown in size and have reached the point where they exert a strong influence on the earnings picture of a utility. An examination of the relationship of the AFC credit and reported net income for all Class A and B electric utilities from 1961 through 1972 reveals that, despite the fact that reported net income was higher for each succeeding year, this was not the case for the AFC credit, although a steady growth was evident. Table 15 indicates that for these utilities as a group the AFC credit from 1961–1964 did not show any particular upward or downward trend, even though net income during this period advanced each year. In fact, this same relationship had existed for the electric utility industry since 1952,[36] but in 1964 a new trend appeared. While net income continued to increase annually, the AFC credit also began an upward movement. In recent years the credit has grown significantly, both in absolute amount and relative to net income. The impact of this growth is evidenced by the fact that, for the A and B electric utilities as a group, in 1965 the AFC credit represented an amount equal to 3.6 percent of net income, while in 1969 this figure had risen to approximately 12.6 percent and by 1972 to 24.2 percent.

The recent growth in magnitude of the allowance credit and its increasing impact on utility net income is even more pronounced when one examines the effect which this credit has had upon many individual

---

[34] Ibid.

[35] Walker, "Interest During Construction Credits," p. 14.

[36] FPC, *Statistics*, 1955, p. xxx.

TABLE 15.   AFC Credit and Reported Net Income, Class A and B Electric Utilities, 1961–1972

Year	Net income (including AFC) credit (thousands of dollars)	AFC credit (thousands of dollars)	AFC as a percentage of net income
1961	1,874,786	84,397	4.5
1962	2,053,477	88,929	4.3
1963	2,178,353	78,881	3.6
1964	2,393,416	85,142	3.6
1965	2,580,688	93,747	3.6
1966	2,749,071	127,480	4.6
1967	2,908,302	186,261	6.4
1968	2,995,525	274,728	9.2
1969	3,195,961	402,878	12.6
1970	3,407,525	588,406	17.3
1971	3,851,995	812,044	21.1
1972	4,419,491	1,068,682	24.2

SOURCE: Federal Power Commission, *Statistics of Privately Owned Electric Utilities in the United States 1972* (Washington, D.C.: U.S. Government Printing Office, December 1973), pp. XXV, XXVII, and XXVIII.

companies within the industry. For example, the June 1970 issue of *Electric Light and Power*, in reporting the income and earnings performance of the leading 100 electric utility companies in the United States, pointed out the following with regard to the Baltimore Gas and Electric Company:

> BG & E's rise to prominence among income producers resulted largely from a change in accounting procedures. In 1969, the company realized the full benefit of charging interest to the cost of new construction. In 1968, the accounting change-over pertained only to the last half of the year. The increase in capitalized interest, more than 3.7 million, resulted in a net increase of 6.7 percent in the interest costs, equivalent to 23 cents of the year's 28 cent gain in earnings per common share.[37]

[37] Robert A. Lincicome, ed., "The Top 100 Electric Utilities," *Electric Light and Power* 48 (June 1970): 30.

In 1969, Baltimore Gas and Electric showed an 18.7 percent increase in net income over 1968. The absolute dollar increase was approximately $7.2 million, of which $3.7 million, or 51.3 percent, was represented by AFC credits. In adopting the practice of capitalization for the last half of 1968, BG&E, in 1969, was able to show the fourth largest growth in net income among the leading 100 electric utilities.

The impact of AFC credits on the net incomes of 203 Class A and B electric utilities is also evident from an examination of their records for the five-year period 1968–1972, displayed in Table 16. These utilities are grouped according to magnitude of AFC as a percentage of net income. A downward trend is evident in the number of utilities not capitalizing AFC. A similar downward movement is apparent in the number of those companies in which 20 percent or less of their net income comes from AFC. On the other hand, the increase in the number of utilities in which AFC comprises 21 percent or more of net income is substantial. For example, only 7 companies had between 21 and 40 percent of their net income produced by AFC in 1968; by 1971 the number of companies had grown to 43—a 500 percent increase. For the five-year period an even more dramatic growth is evident in the number of those utilities with 41 percent or more of their net income produced by AFC; during this time the growth was 950 percent!

An added insight on the effects of capitalizing AFC on net income involves dividend payments to common stockholders. In a substantial number of utilities a sizable amount of actual dividend payments has resulted from AFC credits being added to net income available for dividends. Table 17 displays this information. The figures show the number of companies grouped by that percentage of actual dividend payment provided by AFC credits. Thus, the categories from 1–5 percent through more than 40 percent indicate the number of utilities whose net income from operations available for dividends was less than the total common dividends paid. During the 1968–1972 period, fewer firms were able to rely solely on operations for dividend payments. This is displayed in the "0.0" row, where the number of utilities relying on AFC credits for dividends grew dramatically, despite the fact that such credits are not a source of cash-flow funds.

The statistics in Table 17 present clear evidence that AFC credits have been increasing substantially and, as a result, have exerted a significant impact on electric utilities' net income. This has caused analysts and others to become alarmed over the growth and size of these credits.

TABLE 16.   AFC Credit as a Percentage of Net Income, Class A and B Electric Utilities, 1968–1972

Percentage	1968	1969	1970	1971	1972
No AFC	34	28	29	26	23
—ᵃ	0	0	1	1	1
0.1–5.0	73	69	52	53	58
6–10	46	25	27	22	18
11–20	41	51	46	37	31
21–40	7	26	37	43	49
Over 40	2	4	11	21	25

SOURCE: Federal Power Commission, *Statistics of Privately Owned Electric Utilities in the United States, 1968–1972* (Washington, D.C.: U.S. Government Printing Office, October 1969; November 1970; December 1971; December 1972; December 1973).

NOTE: Net income is calculated including AFC but after preferred dividends.

ᵃ Utility with net loss or payout of preferred stock dividends greater than net income including AFC.

TABLE 17.   Percentage of Dividend Paid Out of AFC Credit, Class A and B Electric Utilities, 1968–1972

Percentage	1968	1969	1970	1971	1972
No AFC	34	28	29	26	23
—ᵃ	20	18	19	27	14
0.0	141	137	123	101	123
0.1–5.0	3	7	5	10	13
6–10	3	3	6	6	2
11–20	1	8	10	15	7
21–40	0	0	6	13	16
Over 40	1	2	5	5	4
Total	203	203	203	203	202

SOURCE: Federal Power Commission, *Statistics of Privately Owned Electric Utilities in the United States, 1968–1972* (Washington, D.C.: U.S. Government Printing Office, October 1969; November 1970; December 1971; December 1972; December 1973).

NOTE: Calculated by: Common Stock Dividends — [Net income — (Preferred Dividends + AFC)] ÷ Common Stock Dividend × 100 = .

ᵃ Utilities with common stock dividend payments greater than net income including AFC.

Some even have used this change in magnitude as a basis for questioning the very soundness of the practice itself.[38] The former chief accountant of the New York State Public Service Commission recently expressed his concern over the present materiality of AFC credits in relation to the net incomes of many electric utilities. After pointing out the large allowance credits firms have experienced, he stated that some companies are able to report greater net incomes from year to year merely by increasing the allowances which they capitalize.[39] Implied in his statement is the idea that electric utilities can use the practice to manipulate their net incomes. He uses this argument as one reason to question the propriety of continuing to allow utilities to use the technique.[40] However, the present practice of capitalizing AFC is necessary and inherently sound. While it is true that the magnitude of the credit resulting from this practice *materially can affect* net income, that fact alone should not imply that the device is being used to *manipulate* net income.

In 1971 the Securities and Exchange Commission, also concerned about the problem, began requiring informally that electric utilities include full disclosure of the details of AFC in their registration statement forms S-1, S-7, and S-9. Today many firms filing these statements show the following details relating to AFC as a note to the statement of income: (1) that part of net income (or the amount of net income applicable to common equity) attributable to the common equity portion of AFC and (2) calculations to support the portion attributable to the common equity portion of AFC as shown in the registration statement.

The following, from an Ohio Edison Company prospectus, is a typical footnote to accompany the statement:

> The allowance for funds used during construction, an item of non-operating income, is defined in the applicable regulatory systems of accounts as the net cost, during the period of construction, of borrowed funds used for construction purposes and a reasonable rate upon other funds when so used. Such allowance has increased substantially since 1968 principally as the result of substantial increases in the amount of construction work in progress and also as a result of increases in the rate of such allowance from 6% to 6½% per annum (effective May 1, 1968); from 6½% to 7% per annum (effective July 1, 1969); and from 7% to 8% per an-

---

[38] Richard Walker, "The Capital Cost of Utility Construction," *Arthur Andersen Chronicle* 31 (September 1971): 30.

[39] Morris, "Capitalization," p. 25.

[40] Ibid., p. 26.

num (effective July 1, 1970). Such rates are based on the costs of incremental capital to the company and companies capitalized or comparable utility companies in similar circumstances.

Assuming that funds used to finance construction by the company capitalized during the five years ended December 31, 1972, were supplied in the same proportion as the Company's average capitalization ratios for the period (i.e., 52% from first mortgage bonds, 14% from preferred stock equity; and 34% from common stock equity), the common stock component of the allowance for funds used during construction as related to earnings on common stock amounted to .2%, 1.6%, 6.5%, 15.5% and 23.2% for the years 1968, 1969, 1970, 1971, and 1972, respectively.

In determining the percentage of common stock component of the AFC as related to earnings on common stock, a number of calculations must be made, the key element being the capitalization ratio. Exhibit 6 illustrates the calculation procedure for the year 1972.

There are valid explanations for the recent large increases of AFC credits in electric companies. First, the growing magnitude of the construction programs undertaken in the past few years by the privately owned firms affect the amounts of reported AFC since the expenditures for these programs represent the bases for the AFC calculation. The rapid growth of construction expenditures is quite evident from Table 18. Note that the $4 billion spent for construction in 1965 was, up to

TABLE 18. Expenditures for Investment in Electric Utility Plant, Privately Owned Companies, 1965–1972

Year	Expenditures (billions of dollars)	Increase	
		Absolute (billions of dollars)	Percentage
1965	4.0		
1966	4.9	.9	22.5
1967	6.2	1.3	26.5
1968	7.2	1.0	16.1
1969	8.3	1.1	15.3
1970	9.9	1.8	19.3
1971	11.9	2.0	20.2
1972	13.3	1.4	11.8

SOURCE: Federal Power Commission, *Statistics of Privately Owned Electric Utilities in the United States, 1965–1972* (Washington, D.C.: U.S. Government Printing Office, 1974).

EXHIBIT 6. Calculation of Portion of AFC Attributable to Funds Provided by Common Stock Equity

Sources of capitalization	Capitalization ratio	Cost rate	Weighted rate	Percentage of weighted rate	Allocation of AFC (000)	Net income applicable to common stock (000)	Common stock equity component of AFC as percentage of net income applicable to common stock
Debt	52.0%	7.50%	3.90%	48.75%	$1,447		
Preferred stock	14.0%	7.00%	.98%	12.25%	363		
Common stock equity	34.0%	9.18%	3.12%	39.00%	1,159		
	100.0%		8.00%	100.00%	$2,969	$4,999	23.2%

that time, the largest amount ever expended in one year by the electric utility industry! These large increases were due primarily to the need for larger generating plants, including nuclear plants, to meet the growing demands for power and the constantly rising costs of materials and labor used in plant construction.

Furthermore, during the past few years the economy has experienced a sharp rise in actual interest costs. Whereas the prime rate of interest in January 1966 was 5 percent, by June 1969 the rate had increased to 8.5 percent, and it has continued at or above this level through 31 December 1974, at which time the First National City Bank of New York quoted a prime rate of 10 percent. The effect of these rising interest rates is to increase the costs of capital incurred by the electric companies. As a result, they are forced to raise their AFC capitalization rates in an attempt to meet the burden of increased capital costs. These factors explain to a large extent what appears to be a disproportionate rise in the relationship of the AFC credit to net income recently experienced by many electric utilities.

AFC AND INTEREST COVERAGES

Because of its impact on the earnings of a utility, the AFC credit also has an effect on the fixed charge coverage calculation. The fixed charge coverage ratio represents the relationship between earnings available for the payment of all interest charges and the total amount of all fixed charges. The best measure of coverage is to use net income before taxes and interest as the numerator in this calculation and total interest charges as the denominator.[41] To the extent that the AFC credit affects the determination of net income or of interest charges in the utility situation, it also can exert a marked effect on fixed charge coverages. Tables 19 and 20 indicate these effects. Table 19 displays by categories for 1972 the percentage changes in coverage if AFC is excluded as part of pretax income, while Table 20 shows the change in interest coverage when AFC is eliminated.

The fixed charge coverage ratio is one of the analytical tools used by investment statistical service companies, such as Moodys and Standard

---

[41] Net income before taxes should be used in the calculation of fixed charge coverage because income taxes are applied after the deduction of bond interest, and it is before tax income that gives protection to the bondholders.

and Poors, in determining the quality of bonds for investment purposes. Although this is only one of many factors considered in rating bonds, the degree to which fixed charge requirements are protected by utility earnings to a large extent determines the rating assigned to a bond. In addition, under the 1933 Securities Act, the SEC, in Form S-9, pre-

TABLE 19.   Percentage Reduction of Debt Interest Coverage by Eliminating AFC from Pretax Income, 1972

Percentage reduction	Number of utilities
No AFC	23
No change	2
0.0–5.0	85
6–10	33
11–15	31
16–20	21
21–25	3
26–30	2
More than 30	2
Total Class A and B electric utilities	202

SOURCE: Federal Power Commission, *Statistics of Privately Owned Electric Utilities in the United States, 1972* (Washington, D.C.: U.S. Government Printing Office, December 1973).

TABLE 20.   Debt Interest Coverage Effects on Times Interest Earned by Eliminating AFC from Pretax Income, 1972

Coverage reduction	Number of utilities
No AFC	23
No change	2
0.0–0.50 times	155
0.51–1.00 times	19
1.01–1.50 times	0
1.51–2.00 times	0
2.01–2.50 times	0
2.51–3.00 times	0
More than 3.00 times	3
Total Class A and B electric utilities	202

SOURCE: Federal Power Commission, *Statistics of Privately Owned Electric Utilities in the United States, 1972* (Washington, D.C.: U.S. Government Printing Office, December 1973).

scribes the computation of fixed charge coverage ratios as part of the requirements for registering nonconvertible, fixed interest debt securities. To qualify for registration under the act, a utility must have a designated minimum fixed charge coverage ratio. Paragraph A (4) of the General Instruction, which sets forth the rules for the use of Form S-9, reads as follows:

> (4) If the issuer has had fixed charges during any of its last five fiscal years or any more recently-ended twelve-month period reported in the registration statement, then (i) the earnings of the issuer, after all operating and income deductions except fixed charges and taxes based on income or profits and after eliminating undistributed income of unconsolidated persons, have been at least three times its fixed charges in the case of utilities, or ten times its fixed charges in the case of any other issuer, for each such fiscal year and twelve-month period; and (ii) for the last fiscal year or twelve-month period so reported, such earnings have been at least three times its fixed charges in the case of utilities, or six times its fixed charges in the case of any other issuer, for such period adjusted to give effect to (A) the issuance of securities to be registered, (B) any issuance or retirement of securities during or after such period, or (C) any presently proposed issuance, retirement or redemption of securities.[42]

Similar provisions with respect to fixed charge coverages also can be found in bond indenture agreements. The indenture usually sets a minimum coverage ratio which, if violated, prohibits a company from incurring additional indebtedness. The fixed charge coverage ratio is a widely used earnings test and one that correlates roughly with bond quality.[43]

A matter of particular concern to those who have had to calculate fixed charge coverages for electric utilities has been the question of the proper treatment of the AFC credit in the computation. This credit never has been applied consistently or uniformly by those who have calculated coverage ratios for utilities. Some analysts completely exclude the AFC credit; others include it as a part of the earnings available for interest; a third group deducts it from the total interest charge. Yet, if

---

[42] Commerce Clearing House, *Federal Securities Law Reports* (Chicago: Commerce Clearing House, 1971), p. 6342.

[43] John P. Childs and Francis Woodbridge, A *Practical Introduction to Public Utility Security Analysis* (New York: Barron's Publishing Co., 1940), p. 3.

the AFC credit is sizable, as has been the case in the past few years, the manner in which it is used in the coverage calculation can effect the ratio markedly. In the case of the Detroit Edison Company, for example, total fixed charges for 1970 amounted to $45,810,000 and were covered 2.58 times by net income (excluding a $16,760,000 credit for AFC) before interest and income taxes of $118,578,000. If the $16,760,000 AFC credit had been deducted from interest charges instead, the fixed charges of $29,050,000 would have been covered 4.08 times by net income (excluding the AFC credit) before interest and income taxes. By including the credit in net income, fixed charges of $45,810,000 would have been covered 2.95 times. These variations emphasize the importance of properly classifying the AFC credit in a manner consistent with its characteristics and with the essential purposes for computing these ratios.

Under the 1958 edition of the NARUC system of accounts and the pre-1971 FPC systems, the AFC credit was classified in the income deductions section of the income statement as a subtraction from interest charges. Consequently, total interest charges were reflected net of the AFC credit. Any fixed charge coverage computed on this basis gives a ratio that fails to reflect an accurate picture of the protection that fixed charges receive from earnings. Classifying the allowance credit in this manner not only is inconsistent with its intended purpose of representing an allowance to the utility for the use of funds used during construction, but also tends to yield overstated coverage ratios as the AFC credit does not reduce directly the interest charges for which the utility is responsible.[44] *Moody's Public Utility Manual* includes the credit for AFC as a part of the company's earnings base and does not treat it as a credit against interest requirements. In this ratio, the credit is treated as "Other income."[45] Although Moody's at one time computed coverage ratios using the AFC credit as a deduction from "Interest charges," it now has settled on the procedure described above.

Consistent with the credit's essential characteristic of representing an earnings allowance to the utility, the credit for AFC capitalized is a proper addition to utility income. This was recognized by the FPC in

---

[44] The proposed rulemaking of the FPC is suggesting a rectification of this inconsistency. See note 4 above.

[45] Moody's Investor's Service, Inc., *Moody's Public Utility Manual* (New York: the Service, 1974), p. xii.

Order No. 436, which moves the credit in the utility income statement from the "Interest charges" section to the "Other income" section.[46] Accepting this approach as correct also requires that, for purposes of computing fixed charge coverages, the AFC credit be included as part of earnings available for interest charges. Graham, Dodd, and Cottle, in supporting this position, state that capitalized AFC is the most practical measure of "earnings" applicable to the nonproductive investment represented by construction work in progress.[47] Consequently, in computing coverage ratios, they assert that the credit should be included in income. This procedure is also consistent with the format specified by the SEC in its requirement for computing coverages under Form S-9 adopted pursuant to the Securities Act of 1933. Under the act, any utility that issues a prospectus for the sale of debt must show ratios of earnings to fixed charges. Earnings for this purpose are defined as follows: "(b) Earnings shall be computed after all operating and income deductions except fixed charges and taxes based on income or profits and after eliminating undistributed income of unconsolidated persons. In the case of utilities, interest credits charged to construction shall be added to gross income and not deducted from interest."[48] As already mentioned, Moody's *Manual* also advocates the same procedure for computing fixed charge coverage ratios.[49]

An opposing view has been voiced by Charles Tatham, who regards AFC as having an element of financial risk. Although an adequate return is anticipated when new construction begins, Tatham believes that since the return is not guaranteed it should be borne only by the common stockholder. Inasmuch as the preferred stock investor and the bondholder are not being paid for this assumption of risk, AFC should not be included in the measurement of coverages for either debt or preferred capital.[50]

Examination of coverage ratios reported for electric utilities reveals that not all of the computations include the AFC credit in the ratios. For example, an article on the subject in *Forbes* used operating income and

---

[46] FPC, *Order No. 436*, pp. 4–5.
[47] Graham, Dodd et al., *Security Analysis*, p. 295.
[48] Commerce Clearing House, *Law Reports*, p. 6345.
[49] See above.
[50] "IV Other Rating Factors, Comments of Charles Latham," *Public Utilities Fortnightly* 92 (27 September 1973): 33.

total interest charges in presenting the ratios.[51] The analysts who calculate coverages in this manner apparently believe that the AFC credit does not represent a reduction of interest charges. In addition, because the credit does not generate immediate cash flow or operating earnings, they also are unwilling to accept it as a legitimate source of earnings for coverage purposes. Although the allowance credit should not be treated as a reduction of interest charges, it is also improper to exclude it from income for purposes of coverage computations. As previously mentioned, the credit characteristically represents an earnings allowance to the utility and, as such, should be included as part of income.[52] To exclude the credit from income in determining fixed charge coverages would tend to understate the utility's true coverage ratio.

AFC AND INCOME TAX ALLOCATION

The vast majority of electric utilities capitalize allowance for funds used during construction for accounting and rate-making purposes. This practice affords them the opportunity eventually to recover these costs through future revenues. In the case where interest capitalized during the construction period actually is paid on funds borrowed to finance construction, the Internal Revenue Code permits the taxpayer to elect to capitalize this interest for tax purposes, despite the fact that under the income tax law all interest payments can be deducted when incurred.[53] Nevertheless, the majority of electric utilities, in computing income for tax purposes, deduct the entire amount of interest paid on borrowed funds, including the interest expense incurred in financing construction. In response to question 11 in our survey, 116 of 125 utilities reported taking the full interest expense incurred in financing construction as a current tax deduction, while only 7 that capitalized AFC for book purposes did the same for tax purposes.

The general practice among the electric utilities for capitalizing AFC for accounting and rate-making purposes while deducting it for tax purposes gives rise to a difference between the periods in which the interest paid affects taxable income and the periods in which this interest enters

---

51 "Ouch—The Utilities Financing Pressure Keeps Rising," *Forbes* 107 (1 April 1971): 41.

52 See pp. 117–21.

53 U.S. Internal Revenue Service, *Internal Revenue Code—1954*, Section 266.

into the determination of income for accounting and rate-making purposes. The difference is that the income tax currently payable for the period is less than what the appropriate tax expense should be in order to match properly the expense with the corresponding pretax accounting income. Normally, when such a timing difference arises between taxable and accounting income, sound accounting theory would dictate that comprehensive interperiod tax allocation be adopted.[54] Yet, an examination of the accounting policies of the utilities revealed that the vast majority of these companies did not follow this procedure. As noted before, the 1970 survey disclosed that only 7 of 116 firms allocated income taxes arising from the differences in the timing of recognizing expenses.

The manner in which the tax effect has been treated by regulatory authorities for rate-making purposes is the major reason why most utilities generally have not allocated income taxes for the tax effect of capitalized interest. In the majority of jurisdictions, commissions have not allowed utilities to include deferred taxes for capitalized interest in rate determinations. Rather, companies have been allowed to recover only actual income taxes payable, which also would include the future increased income taxes resulting from the fact that the deduction had been taken earlier. Since commissions usually have disallowed in rate determinations the recognition of deferred taxes for this item and have allowed the recovery of the increased taxes in future rate collections, accounting recognition for the deferment of taxes has not been required.

This difference in accounting approaches for regulated and unregulated enterprises has been clearly acknowledged by the Accounting Principles Board in the Addendum to *Opinion No. 2*, a portion of which states: "However, differences may arise in the application of generally accepted accounting principles as between regulated and nonregulated businesses, because of the effect in regulated businesses of the rate-making process, a phenomenon not present in nonregulated businesses. Such differences usually concern mainly the time at which various items enter into the determination of net income in accordance with the principle of matching costs and revenues."[55]

---

[54] See, for example, Homer A. Black, "Interperiod Allocation of Corporate Income Taxes," *Accounting Research Study No. 9* (New York: AICPA, 1966); and APB, *Opinion No. 11*.

[55] APB, *Opinion No. 2—Accounting for the "Investment Credit"* (New York: AICPA, December 1962), p. 10.

In discussing the applicability of *Opinion No. 11*, dealing with income tax allocation, the Accounting Principles Board specifically exempted regulated industries from following the opinion when the standards described in the Addendum to *Opinion No. 2* were met.[56] Despite the fact that allocating taxes for the effects of capitalized interest is a generally accepted accounting principle, the consideration of rate-making rules apparently is important enough to warrant sanctioning a departure therefrom. Notwithstanding the board's exception to the income tax allocation requirement, as found in *Opinion No. 11*, the failure to allocate income taxes for the capitalized interest on debt not only violates sound accounting theory, but also is inconsistent with the basic objectives of regulatory accounting and rate-making principles.

As previously discussed, one of the objectives of utility accounting is to insulate utility operations from the effects of nonoperating business.[57] For this reason, the accounting systems separate the effects of construction activities from utility operations by isolating respective costs between utility "Plant in service" and "Work in progress."[58] Since income taxes are an above-the-line expense, any tax effects arising from the capitalization of AFC (a nonoperating item) that are not allocated in some form would increase above-the-line operating income. The effect of this increase could result in present customers receiving the benefit of the tax reduction, while future customers would bear the deferred costs; or, if regulation is not responsive due to regulatory lag, the result could be an above normal rate of return later. This situation is illustrated by comparing columns A and B of Exhibit 7. Column A indicates that, prior to any construction, the returns earned on rate base and common equity are 8 and 10 percent, respectively. In column B, the utility invests $1,000,000 for construction, the funds being financed solely through the issuance of 8 percent notes. Column B shows the effect that the construction program has on operating and net income due to the presence of the interest deduction. In the absence of tax allocation, the tax deductibility of interest reduces income taxes by $40,000, and operating income is increased by the same amount, thereby increasing both

---

[56] APB, *Opinion No. 11*, p. 156.

[57] See p. 9.

[58] Construction work in progress usually is considered a nonoperating item in the sense that it does not enter the rate-making process until project completion, when it is devoted to utility service. Thus the utility is recognized as being engaged in two separate businesses, namely, construction and utility operation.

EXHIBIT 7. Impact of Construction Financing and the Effects of Accounting for the Income Tax Effects of AFC Capitalized on Operating Income and Net Income

	Without construction program (A)	With construction program			
		Gross interest charged to construction (no tax allocation) (B)	Net interest charged to construction (no tax allocation) (C)	Gross interest charged to construction (with tax allocation) (D)	Net interest charged to construction (with tax allocation) (E)
Balance sheet					
Assets:					
Net plant in service	$5,000,000	$5,000,000	$5,000,000	$5,000,000	$5,000,000
Construction work in progress	–0–	1,000,000	1,000,000	1,000,000	1,000,000
Total assets	$5,000,000	$6,000,000	$6,000,000	$6,000,000	$6,000,000
Liabilities:					
Bonds at 6 percent	$2,500,000	$2,500,000	$2,500,000	$2,500,000	$2,500,000
Common stock	2,500,000	2,500,000	2,500,000	2,500,000	2,500,000
Notes payable at 8 percent	–0–	1,000,000	1,000,000	1,000,000	1,000,000
Total liabilities	$5,000,000	$6,000,000	$6,000,000	$6,000,000	$6,000,000
Income statement					
Net operating revenue other than income tax	$ 650,000	$ 650,000	$ 650,000	$ 650,000	$ 650,000
Less:					
Income tax	250,000	210,000	210,000	210,000	210,000
Income tax on allowance for funds used during construction	–0–	–0–	–0–	40,000	40,000
Net Utility Operating Income	$ 400,000	$ 440,000	$ 440,000	$ 400,000	$ 400,000

Allowance for funds used during construction—cr.	—0—	80,000	40,000	80,000	40,000
Income tax allocated above the line	—0—	—0—	—0—	—0—	40,000
Income before interest charges	$ 400,000	$ 520,000	$ 480,000	$ 480,000	$ 480,000
Less interest expense	150,000	230,000	230,000	230,000	230,000
Net income	$ 250,000	$ 290,000	$ 250,000	$ 250,000	$ 250,000
Return on net investment rate base	8.0%	8.8%	8.8%	8.0%	8.0%
Return on common stock equity	10.0%	11.6%	10.0%	10.0%	10.0%

Assumptions:
(1) Rate base: $5,000,000
(2) Amount of additional construction: $1,000,000—disbursed entirely at start of construction
(3) Construction financed entirely through use of 8 percent notes payable
(4) Allowance for funds used during construction capitalization rate: 8 percent
(5) Rate of return on rate base: 8 percent
(6) Income tax rate: 50 percent

the returns on rate base and on common equity. As a result, operating income can be increased solely from construction activities if the tax effects arising from these activities are not handled properly. Even if the AFC is capitalized net of taxes by using a lower capitalization rate which recognizes the tax effect (thus allocating taxes directly to the accounts affected), column C of Exhibit 7 points out that the tax benefit still would accrue immediately as an above-the-line item. Consequently, this procedure still fails to separate the results of operations from those of construction.

The results of properly allocating tax effects, by capitalizing interest on the debt component of construction funds for accounting purposes and deducting currently for tax purposes, can be seen from an examination of columns D and E in Exhibit 7. In column D, AFC is calculated on a before-tax basis without any reduction for the tax effect. Tax allocation is achieved by charging income tax expense and crediting the property account or a deferred tax account in the amount of the tax effect.[59] This entry effectively would remove the tax saving from operating income; it also would pass the tax benefit to future periods by reducing property costs, and thus future depreciation charges, both for accounting and rate-making purposes.

In 1969, the FPC issued *Order No. 389*, which amended its *Uniform System of Accounts Prescribed for Public Utilities and Licensees*. A portion of the instructions for account 409, "Income taxes," was revised as follows: "The Accruals for income taxes shall be apportioned among utility departments and to Other Income and Deductions so that, as nearly as practicable, each tax shall be included in the expenses of the utility department of Other Income and Deductions, the income from which gave rise to the tax.... The tax effects relating to Interest Charges shall be allocated between utility and nonutility operations."[60]

---

[59] In August 1971 the FPC issued a notice of proposed rulemaking under which it would require all companies subject to its jurisdiction to adopt income tax allocation procedures for capitalized AFC. The rulemaking proposed that the tax effects for interest capitalized would be carried to a deferred tax account. This proposal was adopted in *Order No. 530*, issued 18 June 1975. FPC, "Notice of Proposed Rulemaking—Accounting for Premium, Discount and Expense of Issue, Gains, and Losses on Refunding and Reacquisition of Long-term Debt, and Interperiod Allocation of Income Taxes," Docket No. R-424 (Washington, D.C.: the Commission, 6 August 1971), p. 12, and *Order No. 530*, p. 7.

[60] FPC, "Order Amending Uniform Systems of Accounts and Annual Report Forms

In accordance with this requirement to distinguish income taxes relating to utility operations from those relating to nonutility operations, in 1970 a number of firms subject to FPC jurisdiction allocated the income tax effects of interest charges related to construction below the line to an "Other income" account. Under this method, shown in column E of Exhibit 7, the tax effect of the interest capitalized is credited below the line rather than to the property account. Consequently, AFC must be calculated net of the tax effect. This method of tax allocation achieves the same desired result as the procedure described in column D of Exhibit 7 and thus represents an acceptable alternative.

The preceding discussion clearly shows that the failure properly to allocate the tax effects on the debt component of AFC not only is contrary to sound accounting theory, but also violates some of the basic principles of regulation and rate making. The need to isolate the effects of construction from operations for regulatory purposes, along with proper matching of costs and revenues for accounting purposes, cannot be met unless proper tax allocation procedures are applied in both the rate-making and accounting contexts. The state regulatory commissions should follow the lead of the FPC by recommending the adoption of comprehensive tax allocation in accounting for interest capitalized, thus recognizing the need for allowing the tax effects of construction activities to be recovered in present rates.

#1 and 2," *Order No. 389* (Washington, D.C.: the Commission, 19 October 1969), p. 15.

7

Alternatives to Capitalizing AFC in the Electric Utility Industry

The accounting practice of capitalizing allowance for funds used during construction has been used widely by the electric utilities for many years. In principle, capitalizing AFC involves the recognition that the cost of funds used for construction is a legitimate component of fixed asset cost. In practice, capitalization in the utility situation represents the means whereby the firm can recover the cost of these funds and also earn a return for their use during the nonproductive construction period. Notwithstanding the fact that, over the years, capitalizing AFC has been the predominant practice, a number of alternative methods have been suggested for compensating utilities for the costs of construction. Two in particular frequently have been advocated: (1) allowance of a higher than normal rate of return and (2) allowance of construction work in progress in the rate base. In a number of instances companies have utilized or have attempted to utilize these alternatives. Therefore, it is important that they be discussed and analyzed in order to determine their similarities and differences, their advantages and disadvantages. In contrast to the practice of capitalizing AFC, these alternatives are not accounting devices; rather, they are regulatory procedures

149

through which a regulatory body can recognize, for rate-making purposes, the cost of construction funds used by a utility.

RATE OF RETURN ALLOWANCE

One procedure suggested as an alternative to capitalizing AFC is to allow a rate of return above what normally would be permitted in order to compensate the utility for the capital costs of construction funds; it has not been widely used. Of the five respondents to our questionnaire who did not capitalize AFC, none stated that they tried to obtain a higher rate of return. The essential reason for the apparent unpopularity of this procedure is that numerous practical difficulties have discouraged its use by regulatory bodies. First, establishing an overall fair rate of return for a utility is a very complex process. The additional problems of determining construction capital costs, such as significant variations, over time, inherent in the construction cycle and the many types of capital invested for construction purposes, would complicate the matter even further.[1] Second, the higher return rate method would necessitate a larger element of judgment in determining how much the greater rate should be. Third, the procedure would be the least popular among utilities and regulatory bodies from the political or public relations standpoint, the practical aspects notwithstanding. Both utilities and commissions constantly are under great pressure to keep overall rates of return on investment as low as possible. If the necessary dollar returns can be secured in some other way, it is politically advantageous to do so.[2] Undoubtedly, for all these reasons the higher return alternative has not gained wide acceptance by utilities or regulatory bodies.

RATE BASE ALLOWANCE

The second alternative to capitalizing AFC also is a regulatory procedure designed to compensate utilities for the costs of construction

---

[1] Arthur Andersen and Co., *Principles*, p. 9.

[2] Everett Lee Morris, "Earnings of Electric Utility Industry 1966–68 Based on Regulatory Accounting Principles Prescribed by the Federal Power Commission Compared with What Would Have Been Reported if Utilities Had Utilized Generally Accepted Accounting Principles Prescribed by the Accounting Principles Board of the American Institute of Certified Public Accountants," Ph.D. diss., The George Washington University, 1971, p. 80.

funds. This second method is distinct from the first in that the rate base, not the rate of return, is the vehicle used. In essence, this method allows the utility to earn a return during construction if, in a rate-making proceeding, the commission allows current construction work in progress to be included in the rate base. Normally, for rate-making purposes, only assets which are "used and useful" are permitted in the rate base; these generally include plant in service, but exclude construction work in progress.[3] By allowing current construction work in progress in the rate base, the firm can recover the cost of funds invested in construction in the same way it can recover those invested in plant in service. Under this alternative, allowed operating income is increased enough to include a "fair rate of return" even on the capital investment which is not yet performing any public service.

An examination of past opinions and decisions rendered by regulatory commissions and the courts shows full support for the practice of capitalizing AFC. On the other hand, cases which have dealt with treatment of AFC in the utility's rate base have not revealed a similar consensus. In a majority of these decisions, commissions and courts generally have held that construction work in progress must be excluded from the rate base if allowance has been made for AFC.[4] However, a number of commissions specifically have ruled that, for rate-making purposes, construction work in progress is to be included in the rate base when AFC is *not* capitalized.[5]

The most recent development in this area has been suggested by the

---

[3] P. J. Garfield and Wallace Lovejoy, *Public Utility Economics* (New York: Prentice-Hall, 1964), p. 72.

[4] *Re Yonkers Electric Light and Power Company* (1934) 6 P.U.R. (N.S.) 132; *Re Com ex rel. Rosslyn Gas Co.* (1933) 3 P.U.R. (N.S.) 61; *Northern States Power Co. v. Public Service Commission* (1944) 53 PUR (NS) 143, 13 NW (2nd) 779; *Re Pennsylvania Water and Power Co.* (1949) 82 PUR NS 193; *Re Georgia Power Co.* (1952) 93 PUR NS 277; *Re Public Service Co.* (1951) 92 PUR NS 443; *Re New Jersey Power and Light Co.* (1950) 82 PUR NS 554; *Re Southwestern Public Service* (1951) 90 PUR NS 449; *Re Central Vermont Public Service Corp.* (1959) 82 PUR NS 47, 116 VT 206, 71 A2d 576; *Re Appalachian Electric Power Co.* (1953) 98 PUR NS 317; *Re Central Illinois Electric and Gas Co.* (1954) 6 PUR 3d 108; *Re Narragansett Electric Co.* (1957) 21 PUR 3d 113; *Re Central Maine Power Co.* (1959) 29 PUR 3d 113; *Re Wisconsin Public Service Corp.* (1969) 81 PUR 3d 39; and *Re Cheyenne Light, Fuel and Power Co.* (1969) 79 PUR 3d 80.

[5] *Re Republic Light, Heat, and Power Co.* (1942) 45 PUR (NS) 374; *Re Southern*

FPC. The commission has distributed a request for comment on a proposed rule making which would allow all utilities subject to their jurisdiction the alternatives of capitalizing AFC or including work in progress in the rate base. To accommodate this proposal, a number of modifications are suggested in the uniform systems of accounts.

For example, in electric plant instruction 3 the proposed modification of the last sentence of subparagraph (17) reads:

3. Components of Construction Cost.

(17) "Allowance for funds used during construction" includes the net cost for the period of construction of borrowed funds used for construction purposes and a reasonable rate on other funds when so used. No allowance for funds used during construction charges shall be included in these accounts upon expenditures for construction projects which have been abandoned, or upon amounts of construction work in progress equal to that proportion of electric plant in service included in rate base.[6]

In view of this FPC proposed rule making, a recent article suggests: "In particular, a long-standing, fundamental regulatory rule would be swept away: the 'used and useful' principle, which states that customers should not pay for what does not benefit them."[7] Furthermore, counsel for the Public Power Section of the Georgia Municipal Association described the proposal as "a permanent solution to a temporary problem."[8]

A rather unique position in this regard has been taken by the Florida commission in its dealings with the Florida Power and Light Company. In 1955, Florida Power and Light discontinued the practice of capitalizing AFC and began including construction work in progress in its rate base. In a 1957 rate order, the commission stated that the inclusion of

---

Utah Power Co. (1949) 78 PUR NS 432; *Re Citizens Utilities Co.* (1951) 90 PUR NS 46; *Re Lone Star Gas Co.* Cause No. 20805, Order No. 29396, 5 November 1954; *Re Potomac Electric Power Co.* (1959) 28 PUR 3d 206; *Re Iowa-Illinois Gas and Electric Co.* (1958) 26 PUR 3d 369; *Re Southern Union Gas Co.* (1970) 82 PUR 3d 136; and *Re Potomac Electric Power Co.* (1970) 84 PUR 3d 236.

[6] FPC Docket No. RM73-13, "Accounts and Reports, Construction Work in Progress," 14 November 1974, *Federal Register* 39 (20 November 1974): 40787–89.

[7] J. Leslie Livingstone and D. C. Ewert, "Why FPC Should Not Allow CWIP in Company Rate Bases," *Public Power* 33 (May-June 1975): 18.

[8] *Public Power Weekly Newsletter*, No. 75-20 (16 May 1975), p. 8.

construction work in progress in a utility's rate base depended upon factors other than whether or not AFC was capitalized.[9] The commission divided construction work into three categories and, with regard to each, ruled as follows:

(1) Construction designed to reach new customers should *not* be included in the rate base unless consideration is also given to potential revenues and expenses applicable to such customers, because present customers should not be required to pay a return on property intended to serve future patrons.

(2) Construction work intended to replace worn or outmoded equipment should *not* be included in a rate base since its inclusion would require the customer to pay a return on excess plant; if the one is included, the other should be retired.

(3) Construction work designed to improve present service but not replacing old equipment *should* be included in the rate base [emphasis added].[10]

As a result, Florida Power and Light reverted to the practice of capitalizing AFC. In 1962, however, the company notified the commission that it no longer would capitalize AFC and requested a definitive ruling as to what effect, if any, the failure to charge AFC would have on the utility's rate base in future proceedings. In response, the commission issued an order which stated, in part:

The rules and regulations of this Commission are not mandatory in requiring that interest be charged during construction but are permissive in nature, and the management of any public utility under the jurisdiction of this Commission in the exercise of sound judgment, may determine for said utility whether or not interest will be charged on construction.

It is further ordered that for rate-making purposes construction work in progress shall be excluded from the prospective rate base in every case where the utility charges interest during construction. If interest is not capitalized then the amount of construction work in progress on which no interest is charged shall be included in the prospective rate base, but in no instance shall a double return be allowed on money invested in construction.[11]

In 1966 the commission reaffirmed its 1962 position by continuing in

[9] *Re Florida Power and Light Co.* (1957) 19 PUR 3d 417.
[10] Ibid.
[11] Florida Railroad and Public Utilities Commission, *In Re: Treatment by Public*

force the order which allowed companies the option of capitalizing AFC or including construction work in progress in the rate base. It believed that giving the utility flexibility in this area would best serve the public interest.[12] It is to be noted that in 1971 Florida Power and Light again began capitalizing AFC based upon the conclusions of the Florida commission to the effect that, in allowing construction work in progress in the rate base, not all costs were being considered in determining rates.[13]

Most recently, in November 1972, the commission initiated an investigation on its own motion to analyze the appropriate treatment of construction work in progress and AFC by utilities under its jurisdiction. Public hearings were held in June 1974, and an interim order for electric utilities was issued on 28 April 1975.[14]

In resolving the issues as they apply to the electric utility industry, the commission reaffirmed its position in *Order No. 3413*: The allowance for funds used during construction, properly applied to any such investment that has not been included in the rate base, is an appropriate accounting technique that has been a generally accepted accounting principle for regulated utilities for many years. The allowance has been, and continues to be, an appropriate credit to current income and an appropriate part of the total recorded costs of the utility's facilities being constructed."[15]

Furthermore, the commission concluded that the optional provision concept (in *Order No. 3413*) of allowing construction work in progress in the rate base be retained; however, there were two modifications. First, in order to discourage what the commission called flip-flopping between capitalizing AFC and putting construction work in progress in the rate base, the commission required approval in conjunction with a formal rate hearing. Second, the amount of construction work in progress included in the rate base should be equal to or less than a normal, average

---

Utilities of Interest During Construction, and Consideration of Construction Work in Progress in the Rate Base, Docket No. 6655-EU, Order No. 3413, 26 July 1962.

[12] *Re Florida Power and Light Co.* (1966) 67 PUR 3d 113.

[13] "Florida Power and Light Says Accounting Shift Raises Per-Share Net," *Wall Street Journal*, 7 December 1971, p. 6.

[14] Florida Public Service Commission, *In re: Treatment by Public Utilities of Construction Work in Progress and Allowance on Funds Used for Construction*, Docket No. 72609-PU (GI), Order No. 6640, *Interim Order for Electric Utilities*, 28 April 1975.

[15] Ibid., p. 2.

amount outstanding over a reasonable time period. If these amounts were in excess of the average, the excess should receive AFC.[16]

In recent decisions a number of commissions seem to be moving toward the position that utilities, in certain circumstances, should be allowed to include construction work in progress in the rate base as an alternative to capitalizing AFC.[17]

In a Wisconsin Power and Light Company case the state commission noted that staff witnesses suggested that the commission consider the cost of recovery of funds used during construction in current rates and that AFC be recorded only when the ratio of construction work in progress to net investment rate base exceeded a specified percentage or amount. The commission also noted that if such a suggestion were followed, an increase in revenue requirements in addition to that originally requested by the petitioner would be necessary. Staff witnesses introduced evidence which indicated that, notwithstanding the additional revenue requirement, the change could benefit the consumer in the long run. Although the commission could not find reasons for following the suggestion in this case, it did request that further consideration be given in future Wisconsin cases.[18]

---

[16] Ibid., p. 3.

[17] *Arkansas Louisiana Gas Company* (1972) 96 PUR 3d 209; *Southern California Gas Company* (1970) 87 PUR 3d 26; *Florida Power Corporation* (1972) 98 PUR 3d 113; *Robert L. Shevin v. Jess Yarborough et al. Constituting Florida Public Service Commission* 21 February 1973 (*Re Florida Power and Light Company*, Docket No. 9777-EU), 274 So 2d 505, 100 PUR 3d 234; Georgia Power Company, File No. 19314, Docket No. 2536-U, 13 December 1973; *Potomac Electric Power Company* (1972) Case No. 6467; *Potomac Electric Power Company* (1973) Case No. 6658, 1 PUR 4th 238; *Upper Peninsula Power Company* (1972) 95 PUR 3d 63; *Kansas City Power and Light Company*, Case No. 17903, Report and Order, 7 May 1974; *Public Service Electric and Gas Company*, Docket No. 726-562, Decision and Order, 14 March 1974; *Southern Union Gas Company* (1972) 96 PUR 3d 510; *Long Island Lighting Company*, Opinion No. 73-17, 9 May 1973, 99 PUR 3d 457; *Orange and Rockland Utilities, Inc.*, Opinion No. 73-5, 12 February 1973, 98 PUR 3d 335; *Portland General Electric* (1970) 88 PUR 3d 141; *Midland Telephone Company* (1971) 89 PUR 3d 288; *Central Vermont Public Service Corporation*, No. 3502, 28 March 1972, 94 PUR 3d 34; *Wisconsin Power and Light Company*, 2-U-7778, Findings of Fact and Order, 8 March 1974; and *Goodman v. Public Service Commission of the District of Columbia*, No. 73-1345, 25 March 1974 (Potomac Electric Power Company).

[18] *Wisconsin Power and Light Company*, 2-U-7778, Findings of Fact and Order, 8 March 1974.

In fact, in two subsequent decisions involving the Wisconsin Electric Power Company and the Wisconsin Public Service Corporation, permission was given to include construction work in progress as part of the net investment rate base, with the recognition of capitalizing AFC only when the ratio of construction work in progress to net investment rate base exceeded a specified percentage. In the Wisconsin Electric Power Company decision the commission said: "Applicant presently uses a 7.00% interest during construction rate as a means of including in the cost of utility plant investment the cost of capital during the construction period. Under current financial conditions, especially with the adverse opinion the financial community presently holds with respect to interest during construction, it is reasonable and just to limit the capitalization of interest during construction to an amount in excess of 10.0% of net investment rate base."[19] The second decision contained similar language.[20]

The New York commission, in a ruling similar to those in Wisconsin, also found that including construction work in progress in the rate base could be used to compensate currently for the use of construction funds. As in Wisconsin, the New York commission restricted the amount in the rate base to a minimum balance and required the capitalization of AFC on amounts in excess of the construction work in progress thus included.[21]

A long used variation, that of capitalizing AFC along with recovery of construction work in progress in the rate base, has been allowed by a few commissions. This procedure combines capitalizing AFC and including construction work in progress in the rate base on the same funds.[22] Under this method, the utility capitalizes AFC for accounting purposes in the usual manner; in addition, it also is allowed to include construction work in progress in its rate base for rate-making purposes.

---

[19] *Wisconsin Electric Power Company*, 2-U-7908, Interim Findings of Fact and Order, 18 July 1974.

[20] *Wisconsin Public Service Corporation*, 2-U-8016, Findings of Fact and Order, 24 February 1975, pp. 9 and 16.

[21] *Long Island Lighting Company*, Opinion No. 73-17, 9 May 1973, 99 PUR 3d 457.

[22] *New York and Queens Gas Company* v. *William A. Pendergast et al.*, P.U.R. 1924E, 59 1 F. (2d) 351; *Monroe Gaslight and Fuel Co.* v. *Michigan Public Utilities Commission et al.*, P.U.R. 1926D, 13, 11 F. (2d) 319; and *Re Consolidated Edison Co.* (1952) 96 PUR NS 194.

In order to prevent earning a double return during the construction period, the firm, in computing its return requirement, includes the AFC credit in its operating income as part of the realized return. In terms of accounting and revenue requirements, this method yields the same results as merely capitalizing AFC if the capitalization rate used is equivalent to the utility's allowed rate of return.

There is one major advantage in allowing a utility to include construction work in progress in its rate base rather than capitalize AFC, and this partially may explain why some commissions have been less reluctant to accept this practice in more recent times. The prime benefit is that compensation is effected immediately, by generating cash flows through revenues, rather than delayed until the property becomes productive. These immediate cash flows, in turn, could lessen the utility's need for external financing, thus reducing financing costs in the long run.

The New York commission recognized this advantage when it allowed Orange and Rockland Utilities, Inc., to include construction work in progress in the rate base. This was cited in the *Long Island Lighting Company* case as follows: "In Re Orange & Rockland Utilities, Inc. (1973) 98 PUR 3d 335, Opinion No. 73-5, we reevaluated the practice of capitalizing interest. On the record produced in that proceeding, we included $4.13 million of CWIP in rate base out of the $10.5 million inclusion requested by Orange & Rockland. That company demonstrated severe coverage problems as well as a history of earnings erosion."[23]

It is interesting to note that, in contrast to the Orange and Rockland decision, the commission found in the *Long Island Lighting Company* case that the company consistently had earned a reasonable return and had not demonstrated any substantial coverage problems. In addition, the commission pointed out that the portion of LILCO's net income represented by AFC was only half as large as Orange and Rockland's. Thus, the massive increase in construction work in progress which LILCO requested be included in the rate base was, in the commission's opinion, not justified.[24]

The New York commission's attempt to improve the utilities' financial position by using construction work in progress in the rate base in no way demonstrates that the method, from a theoretical or conceptual

---

[23] *Re Long Island Lighting Company*, Opinion No. 73-17, 9 May 1973, 99 PUR 3d 459.

[24] Ibid., pp. 459–60.

standpoint, represents an improvement over the longstanding approach of using capitalized AFC. The approach was used here merely as an expedient to aid a firm in a financial plight occasioned by factors more fundamental than the choice of methods used to compensate for cost of construction funds.

The use of construction work in progress in the rate base, while having an apparent cash flow advantage, still has not gained widespread acceptance. This undoubtedly is due to a number of practical and theoretical defects inherent in its application.

A fundamental utility regulatory concept is that each class of customers should be charged only for those costs of facilities from which benefit is derived. Implied in this idea is the principle that costs incurred by a utility in financing construction must be charged to the ultimate beneficiaries, that is, the future customers who actually will benefit from the use of the facilities. The allowance of construction work in progress in the rate base violates this concept because the burden of payments is shifted partially from future to present consumers. If the amounts of construction work in progress remained relatively stable and continuous over long periods of time, there would be little or no unfairness, as all consumers would share a potentially equal burden, but in actuality these amounts do tend to fluctuate from year to year.

There are those who contend that the inclusion of construction work in progress in a utility's rate base no longer violates this cost-benefit concept.

> In the early development of the industry, large expansions were primarily to attach and serve new customers. Communities and geographical areas were attached and serviced for the first time. Securities were usually issues to finance specific facilities which were associated with specific new groups of customers. A much greater use was made of first mortgage bonds.
>
> By contrast, most expansions in the present day and age are to enable the utilities to provide more and better services to the same customers. In other words, "present" and "future" customers are generally the same people and the argument can be made that construction of additional facilities is in the best interest of the company's customers from the planning and initial construction stage.[25]

A similar conclusion was reached by the New York commission in the

---

[25] Morris, "Capitalization," p. 26.

Long Island Lighting Company case: "The traditional argument that interest on construction should be capitalized in order to prevent present customers from being burdened with costs incurred for the benefit of future customers has less validity today, since a substantial portion of these construction requirements result from increasing demand made by present customers rather than growth in the number of customers."[26]

Although this viewpoint warrants consideration, because of the highly mobile nature of our society there still may be a significant number of consumers adversely affected by the allowance of construction work in progress in the rate base. Consumers who move away from a certain area might never derive any benefit from the construction for which they have had to pay. By comparison, the practice of capitalizing AFC never violates the cost-benefit concept.

There is also a very significant practical defect inherent in permitting construction work in progress in the rate base. Inordinate delays in the regulatory process often cause a lag between the time a utility files for a rate increase and the time a decision is rendered, commonly referred to as "regulatory lag." Its major causes are: (1) constantly increasing commission work loads; (2) inadequate commission budgets; and (3) lack of clearly defined commission policies and standards.[27] If a utility were to depend upon allowing construction work in progress in the rate base to earn a return on its invested funds, regulatory lag might confound the attempt. This would be a problem especially in periods of rising costs, inflation, or widely fluctuating amounts of construction work in progress.[28] In such cases, the particular test period during which new rates are set (ordinarily one year in which costs are considered representative of the future), might not reflect the proper return or cost recovery in subsequent periods during which these rates would have to remain in effect. This would be true unless there were some form of "instantaneous" regulation, which, of course, is very rare.

There is also the question as to whether utility commissions would

---

26 *Re Long Island Lighting Company*, Opinion No. 73-17, 9 May 1973, 99 PUR 3d 460.

27 Phillips, *Economics*, p. 710.

28 As noted above, because of the occurrence of widely fluctuating amounts of construction work in progress from period to period, both the New York and Wisconsin commissions found it necessary to limit construction work in progress in the rate base to specific amounts or percentages of total investment and allow the capitalization of AFC on construction funds in excess of this limitation.

be willing to increase rates sufficiently to existing customers to permit coverage of all costs incurred, especially when a major construction program is undertaken. Including construction work in progress in the rate base would increase rates to present customers, resulting in fully taxable revenues being produced from the portion of the utility's own funds used for construction.[29] Assuming a 50 percent tax rate, the utility customer would have to pay twice the amount necessary to support the construction work in progress derived from equity financing in order to generate a desired return on rate base. Thus, the commission may set rates too low for the utility to recover its costs. This definitely could hinder the company's opportunity to recover its costs and earn a fair return, especially when the firm is engaged heavily in construction.

There are additional defects in allowing construction work in progress in a utility's rate base both from regulatory and legal standpoints. As was pointed out, in regulatory theory the rate of return normally is based upon the investment in property which is "used and useful," and property under construction usually would not be considered in this category. Thus, commissions have objected to a utility earning an operating return on investment before property is actually placed in service, and public utility accounting tries to make a clear separation between utility operations and other nonoperating activities. By permitting construction work in progress in the rate base, commissions in effect would be allowing the inclusion of income from nonoperating earnings as part of operating income, which would prevent separating operations from construction. This would appear to be a direct contradiction of an essential objective of regulatory accounting and of regulation as well.

On the other hand, some commissions have liberalized the meaning of the term "used and useful" to include property not yet completed and in operating condition.

> In its justification of the inclusion of plant under construction in the rate base, the Commission observed that there were alternate methods available, providing no double return was granted the

---

[29] Frank A. Peter, "Interest on Construction—A New Look," paper presented at the Twentieth Annual National Symposium, Federal Government Accountants Association, Washington, D.C., 29 June 1971, p. 3. Furthermore, counsel for the American Public Power Association (APPA) estimates the "immediate average rate increase to wholesale customers to be $398 million, or nearly 18 percent." *Public Power Weekly Newsletter*, No. 75-16 (18 April 1975), p. 2.

utility. The Commission specifically found that funds invested in construction are being used for the benefit of the public just as "funds invested in plant in service," particularly where "the record has demonstrated a continuing need for permanently financing a large construction program." We believe this recitation is sufficient. Funds are not necessarily "used or useful" only when they are currently invested in completed plants. In fact, at least one commentator suggests that the method utilized here which requires utility rate payers to pay construction costs "now rather than later" is, in the long term, the least expensive to the rate payers. This would make the inclusion of plant under construction in the rate base, with its corresponding elimination of capitalized interest, a desirable alternative.[30]

The allowance of construction work also could be in direct contravention to regulatory statutes of various jurisdictions. For example, in the *Lee Telephone* case, it was held that inclusion of construction work in progress in a utility's rate base is in violation of North Carolina Statute GS-133(C), which reads: "The public utility's property and its fair value shall be determined as of the end of the test period used in the hearing and the probable future revenues and expenses shall be based on the plant and equipment *in operation at that time* (emphasis added)."[31] Thus it is illegal in North Carolina to include construction work in progress in the rate base. There might very well be other jurisdictions which have statutes that prevent the use of this practice.

SUMMARY

Three available methods for compensating a utility for its capital costs incurred during the period of construction have been discussed. These include an adjustment in the overall rate of return, the inclusion of construction work in progress in the rate base, and/or the allowance for funds used during construction. As regards a rate of return allowance, there appear to be too many practical and political problems associated with utilizing it as the means for compensation.

---

[30] *Goodman v. Public Service Commission of the District of Columbia*, No. 73-1345, 25 March 1974 (United States Court of Appeals for the District of Columbia regarding Potomac Electric Power Company).

[31] *Re Lee Telephone Company* (1970) 277 NC 255, 86 PUR 3d 371, 177 SE 2d 405.

The second alternative discussed, that of allowing construction work in progress in the rate base, although having the potential for alleviating the serious cash flow problems of the utility, which AFC fails to do, also appears fraught with theoretical, conceptual, and legal questions; notwithstanding that, it has been adopted or proposed under certain circumstances by several regulatory commissions. In fact, it seems apparent that the major reason that construction work in progress has been used in some jurisdictions is solely due to its immediate cash generating implications. This, of course, has significant import in light of the current financial dilemma which is facing the electric utility industry.

It also should be noted, however, that none of the methods has the ability to solve by itself the severe financial problems facing the industry. Furthermore, these methods should not be viewed as panaceas to which regulation can turn to overcome specific cash hardships. The important thing to recognize is that each public utility must be given the opportunity to recover the capital costs of its construction funds.

Appendix A

Survey Questionnaire

Survey Questionnaire

1. Does your firm capitalize *any* interest during construction?

    _____Yes: GO TO   _____No
        QUESTION 2   ↓

    1a. Why is it that your firm does not capitalize any interest during construction? _____

    _____

    1b. What alternative measures does your firm utilize to secure a return on its capital committed to construction?

    _____

    1c. Is your firm planning to capitalize any interest during construction in the future?

        _____Yes _____Not sure _____No
        SKIP TO QUESTION 14, PAGE 4

PLEASE ANSWER QUESTIONS 2–13 IF YOU ANSWERED "YES" TO QUESTION 1.

2. Has your firm ever compounded interest during construction?
    _____Yes: GO TO   _____No
        QUESTION 3   ↓

2a. Is your firm considering doing this in the future?

_____Yes   _____Not sure   _____No

3. What was the rate at which your firm capitalized interest during construction for each of the following years?

   1966:____% 1967:____% 1968:____% 1969:____% 1970:____%

4. What is the basis for the rate that your firm uses in capitalizing interest during construction? (check one)

   a. _____Cost of borrowed money related to current prime rate.

   b. _____Cost of borrowed money related to imbedded cost of debt.

   c. _____Some combination of cost of borrowed money related to imbedded cost of debt and current cost of debt.

   d. _____Cost of equity capital.

   e. _____Some combination of cost of debt and cost of equity capital.

   f. _____Rate of return basis.

   g. _____Other (specify and explain) _____
      _____
      _____

5. Please explain, to the extent applicable, the method that your firm uses in determining the *total amount* of interest during construction capitalized:

   Description of method (including determination of the base to which the rate is applied): _____
   _____
   _____
   _____
   _____

   The period during which interest is capitalized: _____
   _____

   Time limitations: _____

   Dollar limitations: _____

   Types of items, jobs, and property excluded: _____
   _____
   _____

6. What policy changes — if any — are your firm contemplating with regard to the methods used in determining the amount of interest during construction capitalized? (Refer to Question 5).

_____ None, or _____

_____

_____

7. Does your firm capitalize interest during construction on preliminary survey and investigation charges?

　　　　　_____Yes　　　　　_____No: GO TO
　　　　　　　↓　　　　　　　　QUESTION 8

　　7a. At what point in time does your firm begin and cease to capitalize interest on these charges? _____

_____

_____

_____

8. Does your firm capitalize interest during construction on land acquired for construction purposes?

　　　　　_____Yes　　　　　_____No: GO TO
　　　　　　　↓　　　　　　　　QUESTION 9

　　8a. When does your firm begin and cease to capitalize interest during construction on land acquired for construction purposes?

_____

_____

9. Does your firm capitalize interest during construction on land held for future use?

　　　　　_____Yes　　　　　_____No: GO TO
　　　　　　　↓　　　　　　　　QUESTION 10

　　9a. When does your firm begin and cease to capitalize interest during construction on land held for future use? _____

_____

10. Has your firm reported, in the last twenty years, the interest during construction credit in any place other than in the income statement? (e.g., as a direct credit to retained earnings, or capital surplus, etc.)

　　　　　_____Yes　　　　　_____No: GO TO
　　　　　　　↓　　　　　　　　QUESTION 11

10a. What were the circumstances when this was last done?

_____

_____

11. For any projects, has your firm capitalized interest during construction for federal income tax purposes?

     _____Yes   _____No: GO TO
          ↓   QUESTION 12

11a. What are the criteria for determining whether your firm capitalizes interest during construction for federal income tax purposes? _____

_____

12. On construction projects for which interest during construction was not capitalized for tax purposes but interest during construction was capitalized for book purposes, does your firm allocate income taxes due to the difference in the timing of the recognition of expenses?

     _____Yes   _____No: GO TO
          ↓   QUESTION 13

12a. What accounts are used to handle the timing difference?

_____

13. Has your firm ever determined a portion of a project to be in service prior to completion of the entire project?

     _____Yes   _____No: GO TO
          ↓   QUESTION 14

13a. How was the capitalization of interest during construction handled under this circumstance?

_____

_____

ALL RESPONDENTS

14. Has your firm ever attempted to identify funds devoted to construction as to source in order to determine the portion of funds coming from equity capital as opposed to those funds coming from debt capital?

     _____Yes   _____No

15. Does your firm utilize large amounts of short-term loans for construction purposes?

     _____Yes   _____No

16. Has it been necessary for your firm to incur commitment fees enabling it to time the dates of borrowing in accordance with progress made in construction thereby minimizing the costs of financing construction?

_____Yes   _____No: GO TO
        ↓   QUESTION 17

16a. Does your firm treat these fees as

_____An item of   _____An item of   _____Other (specify)
      bond issuance   interest expense   _____
      expense   _____

17. Was your firm capitalizing any interest during construction five years ago?

_____Yes   _____No
        ↓

17a. Was it capitalizing any interest during construction ten years ago?

_____Yes   _____No

Appendix B

Questionnaire Responses

Questionnaire Responses

	Number of responses	Percentage of responses
Question 1. Does your firm capitalize *any* interest during construction?		
Yes	125	96.2
No	5	3.8
	130	100.0
Question 1a. Why is it that your firm does not capitalize any interest during construction?		
Other (miscellaneous)	4	3.1
Interest is expenses	1	.7
Inappropriate question	125	96.2
	130	100.0
Question 1b. What alternative measures does your firm utilize to secure a return on its capital committed to construction?		
Other (miscellaneous)	1	.8
Allowance made for construction work in progress in rate base	3	2.3
Inappropriate question	124	95.4
Response not ascertained	2	1.5
	130	100.0

173

	Number of responses	Percentage of responses

Question 1c. Is your firm planning to capitalize any interest during construction in the future?

	Number of responses	Percentage of responses
No	4	3.1
Not sure	1	.7
Inappropriate question	125	96.2
	130	100.0

Question 2. Has your firm ever compounded interest during construction?

Yes	4	3.1
No	120	92.3
Inappropriate question	5	3.8
Response not ascertained	1	.8
	130	100.0

Question 2a. Is your firm considering doing this in the future?

Yes	4	3.1
No	101	77.2
Not sure	13	8.5
Inappropriate question	10	9.0
Response not ascertained	2	2.2
	130	100.0

Question 3. What was the rate at which your firm capitalized interest during construction for each of the following years?

1966 Rate

4 percent or less	2	1.5
5 percent	10	7.7
5.1 percent to 6 percent	7	5.4
6 percent	95	73.1
Greater than 6 percent	2	1.5
Inappropriate question	10	7.7
Response not ascertained	4	3.1
	130	100.0

1967 Rate

4 percent or less	2	1.5
5 percent to 6 percent	4	3.1

	Number of responses	Percentage of responses
6 percent	104	80.0
Greater than 6 percent	5	3.8
Inappropriate question	11	8.5
Response not ascertained	4	3.1
	130	100.0

1968 Rate

Less than 6 percent	2	1.5
6 percent	42	32.3
6.1 percent to 6.5 percent	9	6.9
6.5 percent	48	37.0
6.6 percent to 7 percent	4	3.1
7 percent	14	10.8
Greater than 7 percent	1	.7
Inappropriate question	8	6.2
Response not ascertained	2	1.5
	130	100.0

1969 Rate

6 percent to 6.5 percent	15	11.5
6.5 percent	34	26.2
6.6 percent to 7 percent	14	10.8
7 percent	40	30.8
7.1 percent to 7.5 percent	3	2.3
7.5 percent	8	6.2
7.6 percent to 8 percent	2	1.5
8 percent	3	2.3
Greater than 8 percent	1	.7
Inappropriate question	7	5.4
Response not ascertained	3	2.3
	130	100.0

1970 Rate

6 percent or less	7	5.4
6.1 percent to 7 percent	13	10.0
7 percent	37	28.4
7.1 percent to 8 percent	40	30.8
8 percent	13	10.0
Greater than 8 percent	10	7.7
Inappropriate question	7	5.4
Response not ascertained	3	2.3
	130	100.0

	Number of responses	Percentage of responses

Question 4. What is the basis for the rate that your firm uses in capitalizing interest during construction?

	Number of responses	Percentage of responses
Cost of borrowed money related to current prime rate	7	5.4
Cost of borrowed money related to imbedded cost of debt	1	.8
Some combination of cost of borrowed money related to imbedded cost of debt and current cost of debt	27	20.8
Cost of equity capital	0	0.0
Some combination of cost of debt and cost of equity capital	47	36.2
Rate of return basis	13	10.0
What state regulatory commission allows	3	2.3
Set by management (judgment basis)	4	3.1
Other (miscellaneous)	18	13.8
Inappropriate question	5	3.8
Response not ascertained	5	3.8
	130	100.0

Question 5. Please explain, to the extent applicable, the method that your firm uses in determining the *total amount* of interest during construction capitalized:

A. Description of method (including determination of the base to which the rate is applied):

	Number of responses	Percentage of responses
Other (miscellaneous)	6	4.6
Prior month ending balance	47	36.2
Prior month ending balance—½ expenditures in final month	2	1.5
Average of month's beginning and ending balance	10	7.7
Month beginning balance plus ½ current month's expenditure	36	27.7
Inappropriate question	5	3.8
Response not ascertained	24	18.5
	130	100.0

	Number of responses	Percentage of responses

B. The period during which interest is capitalized:

Commencement of period

Other (miscellaneous)	11	8.5
Start of construction	58	44.6
On second month of charges or expenditures	3	2.3
From first construction charge or expenditure	29	22.3
Inappropriate question	5	3.8
Response not ascertained	24	18.5
	130	100.0

Cessation of period

When job complete or ready for service	53	40.8
To month end prior to completion of work	1	.8
When placed in service	55	42.3
Inappropriate question	5	3.8
Response not ascertained	16	12.3
	130	100.0

C. Time limitations:

None	25	19.2
30 days	61	46.9
60 days	15	11.5
90 days	8	6.2
6 months	1	.8
Inappropriate question	6	4.6
Response not ascertained	14	10.8
	130	100.0

D. Dollar limitations:

Other (miscellaneous)	11	8.5
None	22	16.9
$1,000	12	9.2
$2,000	9	6.9
$5,000	22	16.9
$10,000	22	16.9
$25,000	6	4.6
$50,000	5	3.9
$100,000	4	3.1
Inappropriate question	6	4.6
Response not ascertained	11	8.5
	130	100.0

	Number of responses	Percentage of responses
E. Types of items, jobs, and property excluded:		
Transportation equipment	66	
Office furniture and equipment	64	
Tools (shop and garage equipment)	60	
Laboratory equipment	59	
Communications equipment	59	
Business distributions (improvements, rebuilds, and relocations and extensions, line work)	26	
Blanket orders	62	
Land	11	
Intangible plant	10	

Question 6. What policy changes — if any — are your firm contemplating with regard to the methods used in determining the amount of interest during construction capitalized? (Refer to Question 5.)

Other (miscellaneous)	2	1.5
None	112	86.2
Time, dollar limitations, and exclusions	2	1.5
Applying interest to all construction jobs regardless of size	3	2.3
Possibility of compounding interest	2	1.5
Inappropriate question	5	3.9
Response not ascertained	4	3.1
	130	100.0

Question 7. Does your firm capitalize interest during construction on preliminary survey and investigation charges?

Yes	50	38.5
No	75	57.5
Inappropriate question	5	3.8
	130	100.0

Question 7a. At what point in time does your firm begin and cease to capitalize interest on these charges?

Begin

Other (miscellaneous)	7	5.4

	Number of responses	Percentage of responses
When charges commence (could not ascertain as to whether this referred to preliminary survey or construction charges)	5	3.8
Commencement of survey	2	1.5
When work order issued	3	2.3
Where there are regular charges for a maximum period up to 3 years prior to construction	2	1.5
When decision made to complete project	1	.8
When transferred to construction work in progress, interest is computed retroactively	8	6.2
At commencement of construction	16	12.3
When charges transferred to construction work order	7	5.4
Inappropriate question	76	58.5
Response not ascertained	3	2.3
	130	100.0

Cease

Other (miscellaneous)	1	.8
When placed in service	25	19.2
When job is completed (ready for service)	14	10.8
Inappropriate question	77	59.2
Response not ascertained	13	10.0
	130	100.0

Question 8. Does your firm capitalize interest during construction on land acquired for construction purposes?

Yes	85	65.4
No	38	29.3
Inappropriate question	5	3.8
Response not ascertained	2	1.5
	130	100.0

Question 8a. When does your firm begin and cease to capitalize interest during construction on land acquired for construction purposes?

Begin

Other (miscellaneous)	11	8.5
Month following first charge or expenditure	1	.8

	Number of responses	Percentage of responses
When land held in construction work in progress work order	1	.8
From acquisition	19	14.6
Commencement of construction	19	14.6
With payment of land	3	2.3
When construction on land authorized by board of directors	4	3.1
First construction charge or expenditure (could also mean first expenditure for land)	15	11.5
Inappropriate question	43	33.1
Response not ascertained	14	10.7
	130	100.0

Cease

Other (miscellaneous)	3	2.3
When placed in service	49	37.7
When job is completed (when ready for service)	25	19.2
Inappropriate question	43	33.1
Response not ascertained	10	7.7
	130	100.0

Question 9. Does your firm capitalize interest during construction on land held for future use?

Yes	3	2.3
No	118	90.8
Inappropriate question	5	3.8
Response not ascertained	4	3.1
	130	100.0

Question 9a. When does your firm begin and cease to capitalize interest during construction on land held for future use?

Begin

Date of first payment (land acquired for construction)	1	.8
Start to capitalize interest when construction is begun on such land	3	2.3
Inappropriate question	122	93.8
Response not ascertained	4	3.1
	130	100.0

	Number of responses	Percentage of responses

Cease

Other (miscellaneous)	1	.8
Ready for service	1	.8
Inappropriate question	122	93.8
Response not ascertained	6	4.6
	130	100.0

Question 10. Has your firm reported, in the last twenty years, the interest during construction credit in any place other than in the income statement? (e.g., as a direct credit to retained earnings or capital surplus, etc.)

No	124	95.4
Inappropriate question	5	3.8
Response not ascertained	1	.8
	130	100.0

Question 10a. What were the circumstances when this was last done?

Inappropriate question	129	99.2
Response not ascertained	1	.8
	130	100.0

Question 11. For any projects has your firm capitalized interest during construction for federal income tax purposes?

Yes	7	5.4
No	116	89.3
Inappropriate question	5	3.8
Response not ascertained	2	1.5
	130	100.0

Question 11a. What are the criteria for determining whether your firm capitalizes interest during construction for federal income tax purposes?

Other (miscellaneous)	3	2.3
Policy is to make book income and taxable income the same for this item	2	1.5
Inappropriate question	121	93.1
Response not ascertained	4	3.1
	130	100.0

	Number of responses	Percentage of responses

Question 12. On construction project₃ for which interest during construction was not capitalized for tax purposes but interest during construction was capitalized for book purposes, does your firm allocate income taxes due to the difference in the timing of the recognition of expenses?

	Number of responses	Percentage of responses
Yes	1	.8
No	118	90.8
Inappropriate question	5	3.8
Response not ascertained	6	4.6
	130	100.0

Question 12a. What accounts are used to handle the timing difference?

Deferred federal income taxes	1	.8
Income taxes, other income, and deductions	1	.8
Inappropriate question	122	93.8
Response not ascertained	6	4.6
	130	100.0

Question 13. Has your firm ever determined a portion of a project to be in service prior to completion of the entire project?

Yes	97	74.6
No	27	20.8
Inappropriate question	5	3.8
Response not ascertained	1	.8
	130	100.0

Question 13a. How was the capitalization of interest during construction handled under this circumstance?

Other (miscellaneous)	5	3.8
Discontinued interest on portion placed in service	83	63.9
Broke project into separate work orders	4	3.1
Interest on entire project was ceased	2	1.5
Inappropriate question	32	24.6
Response not ascertained	4	3.1
	130	100.0

	Number of responses	Percentage of responses

Question 14. Has your firm ever attempted to identify funds devoted to construction as to source in order to determine the portion of funds coming from equity capital as opposed to those funds coming from debt capital?

Yes	21	16.2
No	107	82.3
Response not ascertained	2	1.5
	130	100.0

Question 15. Does your firm utilize large amounts of short-term loans for construction purposes?

Yes	113	86.9
No	15	11.6
Response not ascertained	2	1.5
	130	100.0

Question 16. Has it been necessary for your firm to incur commitment fees enabling it to time the dates of borrowing in accordance with progress made in construction thereby minimizing the costs of financing construction?

Yes	24	18.5
No	103	79.2
Response not ascertained	3	2.3
	130	100.0

Question 16a. Does your firm treat these fees as

An item of bond issuance expense	1	.8
An item of interest expense	22	16.9
Miscellaneous income deductions	1	.8
Inappropriate question	103	79.2
Response not ascertained	3	2.3
	130	100.0

Question 17. Was your firm capitalizing any interest during construction five years ago?

Yes	118	90.8
No	11	8.4
Response not ascertained	1	.8
	130	100.0

	Number of responses	*Percentage of responses*
Question 17a. Was it capitalizing any interest during construction ten years ago?		
Yes	117	90.0
No	4	3.1
Inappropriate question	7	5.4
Response not ascertained	2	1.5
	130	100.0

Selected Bibliography

Books

Backer, Morton, ed. *Modern Accounting Theory*. Englewood Cliffs, N.J.: Prentice-Hall, Inc., 1966.

Bell, John Fred. *A History of Economic Thought*. New York: The Ronald Press Co., 1953.

Bierman, Harold. *Financial Accounting Theory*. New York: The Macmillan Co., 1965.

Bonbright, James C. *Principles of Public Utility Rates*. New York: Columbia University Press, 1961.

Canning, John B. *The Economics of Accountancy*. New York: The Ronald Press Co., 1929.

Childs, John F., and Woodbridge, Francis. *A Practical Introduction to Public Utility Security Analysis*. New York: Barron's Publishing Co., Inc., 1940.

Clark, John M. *Studies in the Economics of Overhead Costs*. Chicago: The University of Chicago Press, 1937.

Cole, William M. *Accounts, Their Construction and Interpretation*. Rev. ed. Boston: Houghton Mifflin Company, 1915.

Couchman, Charles B. *The Balance Sheet: Its Preparation, Content, and Interpretation*. New York: The Journal of Accountancy, Inc., 1924.

Dickinson, Arthur Lowes. *Accounting Practice and Procedure*. New York: The Ronald Press Co., 1914.

Finney, Harry A. *General Accounting*. New York: Prentice-Hall, Inc., 1941.

_____. *Principles of Accounting*. Vol. 2. New York: Prentice-Hall, Inc., 1924.

_____ and Miller, Herbert E. *Principles of Accounting: Intermediate*. 6th ed. Englewood Cliffs, N.J.: Prentice-Hall, Inc., 1965.

Foster, J. Rhoads, and Rodey, Bernard S., Jr. *Public Utility Accounting*. New York: Prentice-Hall, Inc., 1951.

Garfield, Paul J., and Lovejoy, Wallace F. *Public Utility Economics*. Englewood Cliffs, N.J.: Prentice-Hall, Inc., 1964.

Gilman, Stephen. *Accounting Concepts of Profit*. New York: The Ronald Press Co., 1939.

Graham, Benjamin; Dodd, David L.; Cottle, Sidney; and Tatham, Charles. *Security Analysis.* 4th ed. New York: McGraw-Hill Book Co., Inc., 1962.

Hatfield, Henry Rand. *Modern Accounting.* New York: D. Appleton and Co., 1909.

————. *Accounting: Its Principles and Problems.* New York: D. Appleton and Co., 1927.

Hendriksen, Eldon S. *Accounting Theory.* Homewood, Ill.: Richard D. Irwin, Inc., 1965.

Herman, Edward. *History of Economic Doctrines.* New York: Oxford University Press, 1964.

Kester, Roy B. *Accounting Theory and Practice.* Vol 1. New York: The Ronald Press Co., 1930.

Keynes, John Maynard. *The General Theory of Employment, Interest, and Money.* New York: Harcourt, Brace, and World, Inc., 1964.

Kohler, Eric. *A Dictionary for Accountants.* 4th ed. Englewood Cliffs, N.J.: Prentice-Hall, Inc., 1970.

Lenhart, N. J., and Defliese, P. L. *Montgomery's Auditing.* 8th ed. New York: The Ronald Press Co., 1957.

Marshall, Alfred. *Principles of Economics.* 8th ed. London and New York: Macmillan and Co., 1970.

Mauriello, Joseph A. *Intermediate Accounting.* New York: The Ronald Press Co., 1950.

Meigs, Walter B.; Johnson, Charles E.; Keller, Thomas F.; and Moisch, A. N. *Intermediate Accounting.* 2d ed. New York: McGraw-Hill Book Co., Inc., 1968.

Moyer, C. A., and Mautz, R. K. *Functional Accounting.* 2d ed. New York: John Wiley and Sons, 1950.

Paton, William A., ed. *Accountants' Handbook.* 2d ed. New York: The Ronald Press Co., 1939.

Paton, William A. *Accounting Theory.* New York: The Ronald Press Co. 1922.

————. *Advanced Accounting.* New York: The Macmillan Co., 1941.

————. *Essentials of Accounting.* New York: The Macmillan Co., 1949.

———— and Paton, William A., Jr. *Asset Accounting.* New York: The Macmillan Co., 1952.

Phillips, Charles F., Jr. *The Economics of Regulation.* Rev. ed. Homewood, Ill.: Richard D. Irwin, Inc., 1969.

Pyle, William W., and White, John Arch. *Fundamental Accounting Principles.* 5th ed. Homewood, Ill.: Richard D. Irwin, Inc., 1969.

Saliers, E. A. *Accountants' Handbook.* New York: The Ronald Press Co., 1924.

Samuelson, Paul A. *Economics: An Introductory Analysis.* 7th ed. New York: McGraw-Hill Book Co., Inc., 1967.

Schumpeter, Joseph A. *History of Economic Analysis.* New York: Oxford University Press, 1954.

Scott, D. R. *Theory of Accounts.* Vol. 1. New York: Henry Holt and Co., 1925.

Scovell, Clinton H. *Interest as a Cost*. New York: The Ronald Press Co., 1924.

Simons, Harry, and Karrenbrock, Wilbert E. *Intermediate Accounting: Comprehensive Volume*. 4th ed. Cincinnati: South-Western Publishing Co., 1964.

Sprague, Charles E. *The Philosophy of Accounts*. New York: The Ronald Press Co., 1908.

Suelflow, James E. *Public Utility Accounting: Theory and Application*. MSU Public Utilities Studies. East Lansing: Division of Research, Michigan State University, 1973.

Taggart, Herbert F., ed. *Paton on Accounting*. Ann Arbor: Bureau of Business Research, University of Michigan, 1964.

Welsch, Glenn A.; Zlatkovich, Charles T.; and White, John Arch. *Intermediate Accounting*. Rev. ed. Homewood, Ill.: Richard D. Irwin, Inc., 1968.

Wixon, Rufus; Kell, Walter G.; and Bedford, Norton M., eds. *Accountants' Handbook*. 5th ed. New York: The Ronald Press Co., 1965.

Articles and Periodicals

Accounting Questions. "Interest on Construction Cost." *Journal of Accountancy* 49 (May 1930): 388–90.

_____. "Interest Payable During Construction." *Journal of Accountancy* 52 (June 1932): 473–75.

_____. "Dividends Paid During Construction." *Journal of Accountancy* 66 (August 1938): 117–19.

_____. "Interest During Construction." *Journal of Accountancy* 67 (June 1939): 374.

_____. "Accounting for Interest During Construction." *Journal of Accountancy* 73 (May 1942): 466–67.

American Accounting Association, Concepts and Standards Research Study Committee. "The Realization Concept." *Accounting Review* 40 (April 1965): 314–18.

Bickley, John H. "Interest During Construction in Public Utility Accounting." *Journal of Land and Public Utility Economics* 1 (October 1925): 414–24.

_____. "Can Construction Create Income and Profit?" *Public Utilities Fortnightly* 88 (22 July 1971): 29–35.

_____. "The Capitalization of Interest." *Public Utilities Fortnightly* 69 (14 March 1957): 361–72.

Blough, Carman G., ed. "Capitalization of Interest During Construction." *Journal of Accountancy* 110 (October 1960): 80.

_____. "Challenges to the Accounting Profession in the United States." *Journal of Accountancy* 107 (December 1959): 39.

Bolster, Dennis R. "Should Plant Under Construction be Included in Rate Base?" *Public Utilities Fortnightly* 87 (27 May 1971): 25–28.

Chow, Y. C. "The Doctrine of Proprietorship." *Accounting Review* 17 (April 1942): 157–63.

Coughlan, Paul B. "Interest During Construction." *Public Utilities Fortnightly* 86 (19 November 1970): 35–40.

Coutts, Barry, ed. "Interest During Construction." *Canadian Chartered Accountant* 78 (June 1961): 567–69.

———. "Report on Capitalization of Interest During Construction." *Canadian Chartered Accountant* 79 (August 1961): 174–77.

Dahlenburg, Lyle M. "Allowance for Funds Used During Construction Calculation and Disclosure Problems." *Public Utilities Fortnightly* 93 (17 January 1974): 17–23.

Dohr, James L. "Materiality—What Does It Mean in Accounting?" *Journal of Accountancy* 90 (July 1950): 54–56.

Frazer, Robert, and Ranson, Richard. "Is Interest During Construction Funny Money?" *Public Utilities Fortnightly* 90 (21 December 1972): 20–27.

Guthrie, Edwin. "Payment of Interest on Capital During Construction of Works." *Accountant* 12 (13 and 20 February 1886): 98–100 and 112–14.

Gynther, Reginald S. "Accounting Concepts and Behavioral Hypotheses." *Accounting Review* 42 (April 1967): 274–90.

Horne, Henry A. "Inconsistencies in Accounting Requirements of State and Federal Regulatory Bodies." *Journal of Accountancy* 66 (November 1938): 303-309.

Husband, George R. "The Entity Concept in Accounting." *Accounting Review* 29 (October 1954): 552–63.

Li, David H. "Nature of Corporate Residual Equity Under the Entity Concept." *Accounting Review* 35 (April 1960): 258–63.

———. "Nature and Treatment of Dividends Under the Entity Concept." *Accounting Review* 27 (January 1952): 104–13.

Lincicome, Robert A., ed. "The Top 100 Electric Utilities." *Electric Light and Power* 48 (June 1970): 60–61.

Lorig, Arthur N. "Some Basic Concepts of Accounting and Their Implications." *Accounting Review* 39 (July 1964): 563–73.

Morris, Everett L. "Capitalization of Interest on Construction: Time for Reappraisal?" *Public Utilities Fortnightly* 85 (4 March 1971): 19–29.

Olson, Charles E. "Interest Charged Construction: Economic, Financial, and Regulatory Aspects." *Public Utilities Fortnightly* 88 (19 August 1971): 30–34.

"Ouch—the Utilities Financing Pressure Keeps Rising." *Forbes* 107 (1 April 1971): 41.

Owen, Ely. "Interest Credit Versus Plant Under Construction." *Public Utilities Fortnightly* 70 (16 August 1962): 232–33.

Paton, William A. "Interest During Construction." *Journal of Political Economy* 28 (October 1920): 680–95.

Rappaport, Donald. "Materiality." *Price Waterhouse Review* 8 (Summer 1963): 26–33.

Reyer, W. C. "Accounting for Construction in Public Utilities." *Journal of Accountancy* 32 (September 1921): 183–91.

Rydell, Ferd. "Interest During Construction." Part I. *Public Utilities Fortnightly* 79 (11 May 1967): 39–47.

———. "Interest During Construction." Part II. *Public Utilities Fortnightly* 79 (25 May 1967): 22–29.

Sprouse, Robert T. "The Significance of the Concept of the Corporation in Accounting Analysis." *Accounting Review* 32 (July 1957): 369–78.

Stanley, W. F. "New Light on Interest During Construction." *Public Utilities Fortnightly* 46 (14 September 1950): 340–48.

Staubus, George J. "Payments for the Use of Capital and the Matching Process." *Accounting Review* 27 (January 1952): 104–13.

———. "The Residual Equity Point of View in Accounting." *Accounting Review* 34 (January 1959): 3–13.

Utley, John F. "Another View of Interest During Construction." *Public Utilities Fortnightly* 85 (23 April 1970): 34–37.

Walker, Richard. "The Capital Cost of Utility Construction." *Arthur Andersen Chronicle* 31 (September 1971): 30–37.

Walton, Seymour. "Interest as a Construction Cost." *Journal of Accountancy* 21 (July 1916): 67–69.

Windal, Floyd W. "The Accounting Concept of Realization." *Accounting Review* 36 (April 1961): 249-57.

Other Sources

Accounting Principles Board. "Accounting for Income Taxes." *Opinion No. 11.* New York: American Institute of Certified Public Accountants, December 1967.

———. "Accounting for the 'Investment Credit.'" *Opinion No. 2.* New York: American Institute of Certified Public Accountants, December 1962.

———. "Basic Concepts and Accounting Principles Underlying Financial Statements of Business Enterprises." *Statement No. 4.* New York: American Institute of Certified Public Accountants, October 1970.

American Accounting Association, Committee on Accounting Concepts and Standards. *Accounting and Reporting Standards for Corporate Financial Statements and Preceding Statements and Supplements.* Columbus: American Accounting Association, 1957.

American Institute of Accountants, Library and Bureau of Information. "Interest Charged to Construction." *Special Bulletin No. 27.* New York: May 1926.

American Institute of Certified Public Accountants. *Accounting Trends and Techniques.* New York: the Institute. Published since 1947.

Andersen, Arthur, and Co. *Principles Underlying the Capitalization of Interest During Construction.* Chicago: Arthur Andersen and Co., 1953.

Barkwill, Albert C. "Interest During Construction." Paper presented to the New York Society of Security Analysts, New York, 30 November 1970.

Black, Homer A. "Interperiod Allocation of Corporate Income Taxes." *Accounting Research Study No. 9*. New York: American Institute of Certified Public Accountants, 1966.

Blease, Ernest B. "Interest During Construction and Its Relation to Rate of Return." Paper presented at the National Conference of Electric and Gas Utility Accountants, Chicago, Illinois, 20–22 April 1953.

Dixon, Maurice E. "Interest Charged to Construction Credit—Its Impact on Current and Future Earnings." Paper presented to the New York Society of Security Analysts, New York, 30 November 1970.

Federal Power Commission. *Accounting Release Number AR-5*. Washington, D.C.: the Commission, 10 November 1965.

————. *Accounting Release Number AR-10*. Washington, D.C.: the Commission, 11 January 1971.

————. "Accounts and Reports, Construction Work in Progress." *Federal Register* 39 (20 November 1974): 40787–89.

————. *Federal and State Commission Jurisdiction and Regulation of Electric and Gas Utilities, 1973*. Washington, D.C.: U.S. Government Printing Office, 1973.

————. "Order Amending Uniform Systems of Accounts and Annual Report Forms #1 and #2." *Order No. 389*. Washington, D.C.: the Commission, 19 October 1969.

————. "Order Amending the Uniform Systems of Accounts for Class A and B Public Utilities and Licensees and Natural Gas Companies and Certain FPC Report Forms, Concerning Interest Charged to Construction." *Order No. 436*. Washington, D.C.: the Commission, 9 August 1971.

————. *Statistics of Privately Owned Electric Utilities in the United States*. Washington, D.C.: U.S. Government Printing Office, 1955–1972, selected years.

————. *Uniform System of Accounts Prescribed for Public Utilities and Licensees*. Washington, D.C.: U.S. Government Printing Office, 1973.

————. "Uniform System of Accounts for Public Utilities Funds Used During Construction and Revisions of Certain Schedule Pages of FPC Reports." Proposed Rulemaking RM75-27. *Federal Register* 40 (20 May 1975): 23322.

Gates, Ralph F. "Interest During Construction." Paper presented to an Accounting Workshop at the NARUC Convention, Philadelphia, Pennsylvania, 12 October 1959.

Goodbody and Company. *A Comparative Study of the Interest-During-Construction Credit for 108 Electric Utility Companies*. New York: Goodbody and Co., 16 September 1963.

Harnack, P. T. "Mechanized and Expanded Interest During Construction." Paper presented at the National Conference of Electric and Gas Utility Accountants, Miami Beach, Florida, 29–30 April and 1 May 1968.

Hatch, A. W. "Interest During Construction." Paper presented at National Conference of Electric and Gas Utility Accountants, New York, 7, 8, and 9 April 1952.

Madigan, J. B. "Depreciation and Other Aspects of Interest-During-Construction." Paper presented at National Conference of Electric and Gas Utility Accountants, Washington, D.C., 5, 6, and 7 April 1965.

Moody's Investors Service. *Moody's Public Utility Manual*. New York: the Service, 1970.

Moonitz, Maurice. "The Basic Postulates of Accounting." *Accounting Research Study No. 1*. New York: American Institute of Certified Public Accountants, 1961.

National Association of Regulatory Utility Commissioners. *Uniform System of Accounts for Class A and B Electric Utilities*. Washington, D.C.: the Association, 1958.

_____. *Uniform System of Accounts for Class A and B Electric Utilities*. Washington, D.C.: the Association, 1972.

Paton, W. A., and Littleton, A. C. *An Introduction to Corporate Accounting Standards*. Iowa City: American Accounting Association, 1940.

Peter, Frank A. "Interest on Construction—A New Look." Paper presented at the Twentieth Annual Symposium of the Federal Government Accountants Association, Washington, D.C., 28–30 June 1971.

Powell, William J. "Pertaining to Calculation and Reporting of the Allowance for Funds Used During Construction (ADC)." Paper presented at the Iowa State Conference on Public Utility Valuation and the Rate Making Process, Ames, Iowa, 15–17 May 1973.

Sayad, Homer E. "An Accountant Looks at Capitalized Interest." Paper presented at the National Conference of Electric and Gas Utility Accountants, New Orleans, Louisiana, 2–4 May 1966.

Spencer, R. S. "Today's Interest During Construction Practices." Paper presented at the National Conference of Electric and Gas Utility Accountants, New York, 5, 6, and 7 May 1969.

Walker, Richard. "Interest During Construction Credits in the Utility Industry." Paper presented to the New York Society of Security Analysts, New York, 30 November 1970.